MW00441134
BUSY MOMS
Boredom
Busters

rom MOPS

ad Macaroni and Cheese
are for the Growly Bugs and Other Tips for Moms
tting Out of Your Kids' Faces and Into Their Hearts
Loving and Letting Go
Mom to Mom
Meditations for Mothers
A Mother's Footprints of Faith
Ready for Kindergarten
What Every Child Needs
What Every Mom Needs
When Husband and Wife Become Mom and Dad
Little Books for Busy Moms
- Boredom Busters
- Great Books to Read and Fun Things to Do with Them
- If You Ever Needed Friends, It's Now
- Juggling Tasks, Tots, and Time
- Kids' Stuff and What to Do with It
- Planes, Trains, and Automobiles ... with Kids!
- Time Out for Mom ... Ahhh Moments

Books with Drs. Henry Cloud and John Townsend
- Raising Great Kids
- Raising Great Kids for Parents of Preschoolers Workbook
- Raising Great Kids for Parents of Teenagers Workbook
- Raising Great Kids for Parents of School-Age Children Workbook

Gift Books
- God's Words of Life from the Mom's Devotional Bible
- Mommy, I Love You Just Because

Kids Books
- Little Jesus, Little Me
- My Busy, Busy Day
- See the Country, See the City
- Mommy, May I Hug the Fishes?
- Mad Maddie Maxwell
- Zachary's Zoo
- Morning, Mr. Ted
- Boxes, Boxes Everywhere
- Snug as a Bug?

Bible
- Mom's Devotional Bible

Audio
- Raising Great Kids

Curriculum
- Raising Great Kids for Parents of Preschoolers *Zondervan*Groupware™
  (with Drs. Henry Cloud and John Townsend)

MARY BETH LAGERBORG general editor
written by BARBARA VOGELGESANG

GRAND RAPIDS, MICHIGAN 49530

ZONDERVAN™

Boredom Busters

Requests for information should be addressed to:
Zondervan, *Grand Rapids, Michigan 49530*

Library of Congress Cataloging-in-Publication Data

Vogelsgang, Barbara.
Boredom busters / written by Barbara Vogelsang.
p. cm.—(Little books for busy moms)
ISBN 0-310-23997-4
1. Boredom—Prevention. 2. Child rearing. 3. Parent and child.
I. Lagerborg, Mary Beth. II. Title. III. Series.
BF575.B67 V64 2001
649'.5—dc21 2001045379

Published in association with the literary agency of Alive Communications, Inc., 7680 Goddard Street, Suite 200, Colorado Springs, CO 80920.

Interior design by Melissa Elenbaas

Printed in the United States of America

---

01 02 03 04 05 06 /❖ DC/ 10 9 8 7 6 5 4 3 2 1

To my husband, Jim,

and to my children, Nicholas, Libby, and Sarah,

for providing me with the honor

of being called Mom

Contents

Help for Busy Moms

MOMS KNOW THAT NAUGHTY children are often bored children. They have nothing to do, and so their little imaginations take them where they should not go. But the truth is that moms get bored too. Do they become naughty moms? No, not necessarily. But they definitely miss out on the joyful possibilities in everyday life.

Barbara Vogelgesang is one fun mom. She's like your favorite zany mom of a girlfriend when you were growing up. Her ideas for keeping kids happily occupied and full of wonder are fresh and practical. But the best news is that she keeps you, Mom, in the midst of the fun.

It doesn't matter whether you're an introvert or extrovert. Whether you love to have the neighborhood at your house or have quite enough to manage with your own crew. You don't have to have a particular temperament to have fun with your kids. Barbara shows you how to make the most of everyday moments—a thunderstorm, the loss of a baby tooth—and gives you the mind-set to make fun on your own. She offers proactive, boredom prevention—for you and your child.

At MOPS International (Mothers of Preschoolers) we believe that better moms make a better world. To be the best they can be, moms solicit advice from parenting experts and mothers and grandmothers. But sometimes the best help of all comes from other moms who, traveling the same road, have made some great discoveries they're willing to pass along. Thus the series Little Books for Busy Moms was born. We've chosen topics to meet the needs of moms, presented in a format you can read quickly and easily. Like this one. To be better moms, moms need boredom busters!

Mary Beth Lagerborg
Publishing Manager,
MOPS International
(Mothers of Preschoolers)

Personally Speaking

PRIOR TO MY LIFE as a mom I had the thrill of traveling with Ringling Bros. and Barnum & Bailey Circus. Yes, you read that correctly. I was a clown in the Greatest Show on Earth. While I was there, I met families from all over the world and observed their parenting from a ringside seat. Circus families are, in some ways, just like our families, but they have a different focus. They don't worry about laundry, grocery shopping, housekeeping, or cooking. Those chores need to be done, but circus mamas don't think about them day in and day out. Instead, they are passing on family traditions, celebrating moments, and using every experience to educate and bind their families together.

Early in life circus families teach their children their profession. I remember a juggler we worked with who practiced constantly. We would often see his preschooler throwing a ball up and down, "practicing" beside his dad.

Circus children are encouraged to stretch their limits. They are praised for working hard and accomplishing a new skill. The only time I remember a parent discouraging a child from trying something difficult was when doing so would put them in danger. My first year with Ringling all the adults were treated to a private circus starring the circus children. The entire cast showed up and enthusiastically applauded each child's act. After the show, various performers helped mentor the children in their interests.

We celebrated everything on the circus. Birthdays, holidays, different cultural festivities, accomplishments, even animal birthdays were a reason to party. It gave the children of all ages something to look forward to. Believe it or not, life on the road can get just as monotonous as being in one place, especially if that is all you've ever known.

Traveling meant exposure to many wonderful sights. Circus families do their best to take advantage of this. We all knew we might never get to this town or country again. On our time off, many of the families completed chores and practice as quickly as possible to be able to tour around.

Shortly after I conceived my second child, my husband, Jim, and I decided to run away from the circus to establish a home. Suddenly I found my mothering swallowed up by housekeeping, the laundry, cooking, garden chores, and endless running around. When I got together with other mothers, they spent more time discussing presoaking stains than playing with their children. This wasn't why I had wanted to be a mother.

I took the matter to God in my prayer time. He reminded me of those circus families I had spent so much time with. My focus needed to shift. But could it? On the circus our "homes" were so small—trailers, motor homes, and twenty-by-six-foot living compartments on a train. We didn't have as many clothes because we spent so much time in costume. On and on the doubts surfaced, but I was determined in spite of them. I was not going to let my chores cheat my children and me out of the fun of mothering.

I shared my thoughts and ideas with other moms. Many of them shared my excitement. Creativity begat creativity. Soon, instead of new window cleaners, we were discussing new games we had tried. We discovered fun ways to include our children in the activities around our homes. We shared local sights and happenings we could expose our little ones to. The best part of all was that we could do all of this inexpensively. Our children were happier. We were happier. Even our husbands were happier.

Housekeeping, for most of us, is boring. Our children get bored watching us do it; they get weary of hearing us nag them to help. Children get tired of the same toys, the same videos, the same everything day in and day out. Sometimes they get bored for no reason. We don't have to look at our lives as a stretch of days one just like another. Let's bust the boredom and celebrate these common, daily mothering moments. Parenting is an exciting adventure; one in which we are challenged to create marvelous memories, celebrate memorable moments, and have fun with our families. We can do it!

Acknowledgments

THANK YOU, LORD, for enabling me to reach moms through this book. Thank you for being the creative God that you are and blessing me with your creativity.

This book would not be a reality without the support and encouragement of so many dear people.

To my husband, Jim, thank you for your love and keeping the house going while I wrote this book. Thank you for putting up with me while I birthed this book and our third child at the same time. You are as responsible for its completion as I am.

To Nicholas and Libby, it was great fun trying out all of Mommy's crazy ideas, the ones that worked and the ones that didn't. Thanks for being such willing guinea pigs. To Sarah, thanks for waiting to be born until I finished most of my writing and for being a baby who sleeps through the night.

To Carol Kuykendall, Mary Beth Lagerborg, and all my friends at MOPS International, thanks for your support, encouragement, and vision. Thank you to all the moms I've met through MOPS who are my fellow travelers in this mothering journey.

To Sandy Vander Zicht and the staff at Zondervan, thanks for your guidance and help.

And last, big hugs to my family and friends who cheered me on along the way. You've been a great pep squad. Thank you to Sally Shane and my ladies' Bible study group, who prayed me through this entire project. All of you are so precious to me.

CHAPTER 1

Beat Boredom With an Attitude of Celebration

CHILDREN ARE SPONTANEOUS creatures who live in the now. They are really good at openhearted, spontaneous joy. They don't put it on hold; anyone who has been lucky enough to receive a muddy hug or a sticky kiss knows that. Children spend joy with abandon. They know the more joy you spread, the more you will have. Children are pros at the art of celebration. They practice it at every occasion. Why shouldn't parents join the party?

Shift Your Focus

We have all heard that a child's work is play. Unfortunately, we often rush past our children's—and our own—need to play. We move too fast and miss life as it was intended to be experienced. Sometimes we need to shift our focus, to look past the surface and see the whole of life, not just today. It's so hard not to let our to-do list or outside appointments keep us from snuggling, tickling, and telling bad knock-knock jokes. The reality is that years from now we'll remember the knock-knock jokes and will have long forgotten what was on those lists.

This shift in focus is crucial when we become parents. My friend Erica and her husband, Andrew, adopted two- and four-year-old brothers. She was telling me how neat it is to see Andrew relax because of these little guys. They have hardwood floors in their house, and Andrew had treated them like fine furniture. Now that he has these sons, he's on the floor pushing Tonka trucks over those same floors. Being connected to his sons is much more important than keeping scratches off the floor.

Make Ordinary Occurrences Extraordinary

Boredom can rob a person of joy. When my children get bored and I get bored, life in our house isn't so pleasant. That's when I look for ways to make ordinary occurrences extraordinary.

When my son, Nick, was five, he had a problem finding things. I would send him to his room to get something and he always came back saying he couldn't find it. There were too many other things to think about and look at on the way from the kitchen to his room. This drove me crazy.

I explained to Nick what a detective was and how detectives solved mysteries and found lost items. We discussed looking for clues and following up on them. I bought an old fedora hat at a yard sale, made a sign that said "We leave no stone unturned," and encouraged him to open his own private investigation agency.

When I needed him to find his shoes, I asked him to help me solve a mystery and formed my request like a missing person's report. He loved it and was able to be more helpful to me. Other times I've been known to send out a knight in shining armor to accomplish a quest. Sometimes it's been, "Your mission, should you choose to accept it . . ." Suddenly, chores were much more fun for all of us.

Encourage Your Children to See the World in a Unique Way

Find ways to encourage your children to see the world in a more interesting, exciting, and fun light.

Make something as mundane as folding the laundry a game. I told my children a story about how the socks got all mixed up in the dryer and how sad they were that they couldn't find their buddies. Nick and Libby were eager to help. They sorted all the socks while I folded the rest of the laundry. What was once a chore became a game we played together.

Liz, a mother of four, had her children use "sock monsters" to eat up all the dust on their furniture. She used a permanent marker to draw faces on several old socks. Each child wore a sock on one hand and used it to dust the tables and dressers in their home.

Forge Relationships with Your Children Now

My husband and I schedule regular "date nights" with our children. On a date night, Libby and her daddy go out together. It may be something simple like McDonald's and a movie. They have time alone to talk, and Jim models how a future date should treat her. He opens doors, pulls out her chair, and gets her coat for her. Nicholas and I share similar evenings. I let him open doors for me and pay the bill at the restaurant we go to. We also rearrange the couples to girls/boys night out. Libby and I may get our hair done, while Nick explores the hardware store with Jim.

The main idea is to get alone with each child every once in a while. Relationships are built on time spent together sharing similar interests and shared experiences. Now is the time to forge relationships with these people who may become your best friends someday.

Create Memories, not Regrets

The Bible tells us that Jesus' mother, Mary, held many things in her heart. I am sure those memories helped her get through Jesus' suffering. Hide things in your heart now. When my children get married or move off to college, I want to have memories, not regrets. Shoulda, woulda, and coulda are sad things.

Since Libby was born, I've been writing her a letter in her baby book. Each year on her birthday or when a special moment happens I jot down my thoughts. It's nothing elaborate, just an ongoing message of my love and pride. I reread it each time I make a new entry. I see her development, and it delights and encourages me. Someday when she is older I will give it to her. It is the history of our relationship, a log of memories. It is a treasure only I can leave for her.

Cultivate a Spirit of Celebration

When Libby was three she was terrified of thunderstorms. I prayed, "Lord, how can I use this to celebrate your power?" We made popcorn, gathered together in a dark room with seats around a window, and used the storm as a show where we cheered the awesome power of God with each thunderclap. Now thunderstorms are a reason to party.

Get to Know Your Children

The more time I spend with my children, the better I know them. I listen to them and ask lots of questions. I also do a lot of explaining. I work at knowing their personalities. What's really going on when they are disobedient, cranky, or bored? Is it a sign they need more of me? What are their limits and abilities? Am I asking them to do more than they can or less than holds their interests? When did they eat last? Are they tired? Are they getting the silent "I don't care" message by my not making special time for them? It is crucial that we spend this getting-to-know-you time with our children.

Don't Be Afraid of Not Being Good Enough

When she was three, Libby began going to a dancing school near our house. Miss Shirlene had a small studio in her barn. The girls twirled and rocked and leaped for one hour a week. Libby didn't learn much dance, but she learned to love the music.

Miss Shirlene modeled creativity and confidence to these preschoolers.

The next summer we sent Libby to a highly recommended, expensive gymnastics school that prepared Olympic hopefuls. It was a terrible experience for our daughter. Libby didn't make any friends, didn't learn anything, and felt very clumsy. The pros didn't know what Miss Shirlene knew: Preschoolers need to experiment with activities to develop their creativity. They need to have fun and make friends. They need to be given potential, not limitations in learning and in life experiences. You don't need to be an expert or professional in any given field to teach your child. You are an expert on your child.

Share Your Interests with Your Children

Childhood should be a happy and satisfying season of life for mothers as well as children. Share your interests with your little ones. You don't need to listen to "children's" music all the time. Nick and Libby love when I play my old rock and roll cassettes. It's probably because they know I'm going to kick off my shoes and dance right along with them.

Involving your children in the things you love will be much more fun for you than trying to keep them busy. My friend Ginny loves crafting. When she works on her projects, she gives her girls their own supplies and they happily work beside her. Sure, it often takes longer for her to get something done, but her girls feel so special being included in Mommy's world.

Be Aware of Those Cranky Times of the Day

The hour from four to five o'clock had become an awful time in our house. The kids were often tired and bored, and I found myself running out of energy and patience. All of us were at the point of needing a soothing break, but a nap would ruin bedtime. Baths calmed my children, so I decided to prepare a bubble bath for them and put on some classical music for me. Next I lit candles, out of the children's reach, of course. While they splashed, I sat on the floor next to the tub and relaxed. It lasted maybe twenty minutes, but it was wonderful.

Candlelight is a magical thing. It makes children whisper and signals to them that this is special. Dinners by candlelight are very popular in our home. Candlelight automatically makes even meatloaf a celebration.

Look for Creative Ideas for Your Family

I've made it my business to look for creative ideas I can adapt for our family. Each one of us has the creativity to be the best parents for our children. Each one of us was made in the image of the ultimate Creator and therefore is creative. I hope the ideas in this book will get your creative juices flowing. Get together with other moms and share ideas about dealing with family situations creatively. As you get to know your kids better, you'll get better at coming up with ideas to suit them. As the *Magic School Bus*'s Miss Fizzle says, "Take chances; get messy."

CHAPTER 2

Tools of the Trade

WHETHER WE DO our work in the kitchen, office, or shop, our job is much easier if we have the correct tools. It's much more efficient to put in a screw with a screwdriver than with a butter knife. Children need the correct tools to learn and develop skills, and it is a big help if you don't have to run to the store every time you want to occupy your child. With this in mind, I've listed several supplies I've found to be very helpful when the "I'm bored blues" hit. These items are not expensive or fancy, they're just the basics. It is also not an exhaustive list. As you get to know your children better, you will be able to provide the supplies that interest them the most.

A Library Card

The most effective tool to open a world of books, audios, videos, and computers to your child is also one of the least expensive items. A library card is free and easy to obtain. Children love having their own library cards. Get one for everyone in the family. We have a designated tote bag for items we borrow from the library so we don't misplace books that do not belong to us. Perhaps each child could decorate a canvas tote bag for their library books. Teach your children to take good care of library books, and keep them all in one place at home.

Kitchen Items to Have On Hand

When you need to have an impromptu celebration, it helps to have the basics in your kitchen. Your family will think you are amazing when you whip up a treat with no warning.

Here is a list of some of the items you may want to keep on hand:

flour
milk
oil
eggs
sugar
baking powder
unsweetened cocoa

baking soda
shortening
vanilla extract
margarine
cinnamon
powdered sugar
yeast
chocolate chips
peanut butter

Items to Save for Crafts

Save these items to use in projects. Only save a couple—you don't need fifteen toilet paper rolls. Every family has a constant supply of these things:

margarine tubs with lids
aluminum pie plates
empty toilet paper rolls
paper grocery bags
coffee cans with lids
shoe boxes
plastic drink containers
newspapers

Craft Supplies

Craft supplies make great children's gifts. I find it's better to give supplies than a complete craft kit. I like to challenge my children's creativity. It's fun to see what they will make as opposed to having them copy what's on a box.

Purchase good supplies. Crayola crayons and a pair of good scissors will help keep frustration levels low. It's so hard to do a good job when your crayon is all wax and no color. Try to store craft supplies in a neat but easily accessible place. When Nick and Libby were small, they had to ask permission to get the craft supplies out.

Plastic bins and shoe boxes make great storage containers for your supplies. If you label the containers with pictures, your children will be more helpful when it is time to clean up. The following is a list of craft supplies you should have on hand:

crayons
washable markers
pencils
erasers
pencil sharpener
butcher paper or newsprint on a roll
child safety scissors
tape: scotch, packing, and masking
white school glue and glue stick
waxed paper
tissue paper
cardboard or poster board
construction paper

pipe cleaners
scrap paper
buttons
rubber bands
yarn
paper plates
bits of material, lace, and feathers
stamps and washable stamp pad
iron
rolling pin
play dough or clay
water-based poster paint
brushes
sidewalk chalk

You will also want to have craft smocks to keep your little ones from soiling their clothes. Dad's old shirt or an apron work well. You can cover tables or floors with newspaper or vinyl tablecloths to protect them from spills.

Dress-Up Trunk

Dress-up clothes have been some of the most used items in our house. Get a large cardboard box and let the kids decorate it for this purpose. You can also use a plastic crate. Start the collection with some of your old dresses and your husband's old shirts and jackets. Garage and estate sales and Goodwill stores are great places to pick up more items. Many stores also sell costumes for up to 75 percent off the day after Halloween.

Here are some suggestions for your box:

hats
large scarves
colorful shirts
bridesmaid dresses
costume jewelry
nightgowns
vests
wigs
boots
shoes
purses
capes
shawls
gloves
aprons

Most children love hats. Look for ones that identify a certain occupation: firefighter, construction worker, nurse, baseball player, football player, or train engineer. Add a crown, animal ears, and a top hat, and you will be able to conjure up hours of imaginative play.

Now that you are well equipped, you are ready to battle boredom in your home. I hope the ideas included in this book will spark your imagination. Childhood is so special, and we, as moms, are blessed to be able to experience it again through our children.

CHAPTER 3

Seasonal Boredom Busters

EACH SEASON OF THE YEAR comes with its own reasons to celebrate. Whenever I ask my children which season is their favorite, they always mention the one we are in. It's such a delight to share the world with these little people who inspire me to applaud the passing of time. Celebrating the uniqueness of each season will help you and your children see beyond schedules and chores.

THE FIRST SNOWFALL

The first snowfall of the winter is a much anticipated event around our house. It holds a magic all its own. The common reaction to snow for any parent is dread. What will we do stuck inside with the kids? But if you look at snow through the eyes of your child, you will see a winter wonderland. The first snowfall, or any time we get snowed in, is time for us to stop what we're doing and enjoy this seasonal delight.

Snow Angels

When was the last time you laid in the snow and made snow angels? Have you ever shown your little ones how to do it? It's great fun to lie in the snow and listen to it crunch as you wave your arms and legs back and forth. The real trick is to get up carefully without ruining the impression left in the snow. Sure, you get all wet, but that's when you need to come inside, put on something snuggly, throw the wet clothes in the dryer, and enjoy hot cocoa with a story. One of our favorites is *The Wild Toboggan Ride* by Suzan Reid.

Ice Luminaries

My husband, Jim, often got home after dark in the winter, and the kids and I wanted something special to welcome him home one frosty evening. We made ice luminaries and placed them all over our deck to greet him. If the weather is right, ice luminaries can last quite a while. To make an ice luminary, you will need empty plastic margarine tubs, spray vegetable coating (like Pam), water, and votive candles.

Spray the margarine tubs with a thin coating of vegetable spray and fill with water. Place the tubs outside in freezing temperatures for about four to five hours. When the water is partially frozen, scoop out the middle. Put the tubs back outside until the ice freezes solid. If it's not cold enough outside, you can freeze them in your refrigerator's freezer. Remove the frozen luminary from the margarine tub and place a votive candle inside it. (If you can't find votive candles, tea light candles work well also.) The danger of fire is small because these candles are surrounded by ice that will melt and put out any flame that gets too hot. Position the luminaries on your porch or deck or line the walk or driveway with them. At sunset, an adult should light the candles, and everyone can enjoy the glow.

Ice Bubbles

It's often fun to do something out of its traditional season. Try blowing bubbles on a cold winter day. They freeze in midair! It's fun to try to catch these frozen ice bubbles.

For great bubbles, mix 1 cup Joy or Dawn dishwashing liquid, 2 cups warm water, and 3–4 teaspoons glycerin (found in drugstores).

Snow Candy

This old-fashioned treat dates back to pioneer days. Adults can watch the molasses bubble while the children ready the pans.

Snow Candy

For 3/4 pound of candy you will need:

3/4 cup dark molasses
1/2 cup brown sugar
4 9-inch pie pans
1 large saucepan
1 glass of cold water
1 6-ounce Pyrex or heat-proof pitcher

Have the children fill the pie pans with fresh snow, then set them outside in the snow to chill while you are cooking. Combine the molasses and brown sugar in the saucepan and bring to a boil. Over medium heat continue cooking, stirring frequently to prevent burning. After five minutes, begin testing the syrup by dripping some from a spoon into a glass of cold water. The syrup is ready when the drops form a firm ball in the water (245°). Pour the hot syrup into the pitcher while the children get the pans of snow from outside. Working rapidly, pour hot syrup onto the cold snow. When it has hardened, break it into bite-size pieces and enjoy.

Real Hot Cocoa

If you've never had hot cocoa made with milk and cocoa powder, you are in for a real treat. It's so rich and delicious, you don't even need cookies! We love it so much we even bought special snowman mugs to enjoy it in.

Real Hot Cocoa

For four servings you will need:

1/2 cup granulated sugar
1/3 cup cocoa powder
4 cups milk
1 teaspoon vanilla
marshmallows

Stir together the sugar and cocoa powder in a saucepan. Gradually stir in 1/3 cup milk to make a paste. Stir in remaining milk. Warm over medium heat, stirring constantly, until hot but not boiling. Remove from heat and add vanilla. Serve warm with marshmallows.

April Fools' Day

Most people either do not celebrate April Fools' Day or they spend it playing practical jokes on unsuspecting victims. In a house full of clowns, April Fools' Day takes on a new meaning! It's a day to be ridiculous. It's a day we honor the fine art of being a comedian, and, as the saying goes, "Everyone thinks he's a comedian."

Dressing Up

The attire for April Fool festivities should be silly. Have kids dig through the dress-up box for wigs, hats, shoes, pants, and dresses, and put together their clown costumes. Make funny hats using paper plates and ribbons or pots and pans. Let your imagination run wild. Anything goes as long as it's silly.

Face Painting

For some reason, kids love to have their faces painted. There is not much to doing it, and the cleanup is easy enough to let them do it themselves. All you need is nontoxic watercolor poster paint, brushes, water, paint smocks, and a mirror. The paint smocks are crucial because it's difficult to get the paint out of material, although it easily washes off skin. It is also best to shake the paint jars and give the children just the paint caps to dip their brushes in. That way there is less for them to spill.

Once everyone is appropriately dressed, allow each member of the family to have their chance to shine in the family spotlight. Tell jokes, lip-sync to funny songs, or act out silly stories. This is the opportunity to teach your children all those "why the chicken crossed the road" jokes. After the family show is over enjoy a snack and some comedy greats. Clowns like Lucille Ball, the Three Stooges, and Laurel and Hardy always get a laugh out of us. The best source for these video classics is your local public library.

Funny Cake

This Pennsylvania Dutch treat is a great snack to have while watching your favorite comedy classics.

Funny Cake

2 unbaked prepared pie shells

Cake:

2 eggs
1 1/2 cups sugar
1/2 cup butter or shortening
1 cup milk
2 cups flour
2 teaspoons baking powder
1 teaspoon vanilla

Syrup:

1 cup sugar
1/2 cup cocoa
3/4 cup boiling water
1 teaspoon vanilla

Mix syrup ingredients and pour into uncooked prepared pie shells. Mix cake ingredients and pour directly over syrup. Bake at 350°

for 35 minutes or until firm. You can also substitute applesauce for the syrup for a fruit version of this snack.

First Day of Spring

I love spring. It's exciting to see all the signs of new life. The first day of spring is not usually spring-like for our family here in the Northeast, but we celebrate the coming warm weather anyway.

Libby is always most eager for spring because she loves picking strawberries. On the calendar we draw a big red dot on the day we think the local strawberry farm will open. She crosses off the days as she waits. The anticipation of one of her favorite outings makes the event even more fun.

Spring makes everyone think of growing plants and flowers. The following two activities will help develop your child's interest in these areas before they actually get into the garden.

Eggshell Sprouts

To make eggshell sprouts you will need: play dough, empty eggshells with top 1/4 broken off, damp cotton balls, alfalfa seeds, felt markers.

Have the children mold egg cups out of the play dough. Set the empty eggshells in the play dough, with the broken part of the shell at the top. Use markers to decorate the eggshells. (If they draw faces on the shells, they can later give their "eggheads" a "haircut.") Place three to four damp cotton balls in each eggshell. Sprinkle seeds over the cotton. Keep the cotton damp, and in the next three or four days the seeds will sprout. Keep the eggshell in a sunny spot, and as the sprouts grow you can enjoy the clippings on salads or sandwiches.

Flower Presses

My daughter Libby loves to gather and press flowers. She finds beauty in even the weeds. After they are all dried in a flower press, she uses her pressed treasures to make cards for her grandma. Store-bought flower presses can be expensive, so we made ours out of some scrap wood.

Materials: 2 pieces of 10 x 10 x 1/4-inch wood, 4 bolts 3–4 inches long, 4 wing nuts, drill, cardboard, blotting paper (we've used construction paper), sandpaper.

This is a great "get Dad involved" project. He can cut the wood and drill holes through each of the four corners on both pieces of wood. Make sure the holes line up, then sand the wood to remove any rough edges. We always let our little ones do the sanding and then go over it to make sure the surfaces are smooth. Insert the bolts through one piece of wood with the bolts extending up. Cut cardboard and blotting paper to fit inside the press. Place one piece of cardboard on the wood. Layer blotting paper, items you want to press, another piece of blotting paper and another piece of cardboard. We have gotten as many as ten layers in our press. The more you put in the press, the longer it will take to dry. When all your flowers and leaves are in the press, place the top piece of wood onto the four extended bolts and tighten the wing nuts. The flowers should be ready in about three weeks.

To use your pressed plants for cards or artwork, thin white glue with a little water. Let your child paint the glue onto the cardboard or paper they are decorating and arrange their flowers on top. Paint another layer of glue over the entire picture. The glue will dry clear and the plants will be secure. Send the completed artwork to friends and family to announce the arrival of spring.

May Day

The first day of May is a fun day for us. We prepare baskets of flowers, real or crafted, to share with our neighbors. The kids love creeping up to neighbors' doors and leaving their surprises. They ring the doorbell and run. We hide in the bushes to see the reaction to our anonymous gift. I think it's important for kids to experience the thrill of giving in secret.

Baskets

We have made baskets out of some of the strangest materials. Making the most creative basket has become part of the fun. Use ribbon to decorate the plastic baskets strawberries come in. Decorate toilet paper rolls and staple them shut at one end, then loop some string or ribbon to make a handle and staple it to the top. Just about anything can be painted or covered with your child's artwork. Try milk containers, old flowerpots, paper cups, or yogurt containers.

Flowers

Materials: White or colored tissue paper, markers, spray bottle filled with water, and pipe cleaners.

If you aren't able to find enough flowers to fill your baskets, tissue paper flowers are easy to fashion and look quite colorful. You can use colored tissue paper or have your children draw on white tissue paper with markers. If you have your children draw on white tissue paper, mist the tissue lightly afterward with a spray bottle of water and the colors will run into each other, creating a unique effect. When the tissue is dry, layer three pieces on top of each other. Fold the layered tissue back and forth on itself like a fan, then tightly secure a pipe cleaner around the middle of the tissue paper. Spread out the tissue paper for a lovely flower. You can make butterflies the same way using coffee filters.

Flower Cookies

To make these beautiful cookie reminders of spring you will need:

refrigerated butter cookie dough
(like Pillsbury)
large marshmallows
colored sugar
colored icing

Slice the cookie dough and bake as directed. While cookies are baking, slice the marshmallows crosswise into four pieces. Put different colored sugars into small bowls and let the children press the edges into colored sugars. Set aside.

When the cookies are baked and cooled, spread icing on cookies. Even little ones can help with this if you let them use the back of a spoon to do the spreading. Place six sugar-dipped marshmallow slices evenly around the edge of each cookie.

Planting a Garden

May Day is usually when we get our garden ready for planting. Check to see when it is frost-safe in your area of the country. I love playing in the dirt with the kids. We put on our old clothes and jump right in. We've had some neat designs in our gardens. We've had a pizza garden, in which we planted everything we like on pizza: tomatoes, peppers, basil, garlic, and onions. My son is not a vegetable eater naturally, but I find if he grows it, he's more likely to eat it—even broccoli and spinach. Try these garden projects.

Flower House

Materials: sunflower seeds, morning glory seeds.

Plant the sunflower seeds in a three-sided square formation about eight inches apart. Plant a morning glory between each sunflower. As the flowers grow your children will have a three-sided "house" to play in. The morning glories will use the sunflower stems as a trellis. Train the morning glories to cross over the top of your "house" for a roof.

Green Bean Tepee

Materials: 3 wooden poles about 8 feet long, rope, climbing green bean seeds.

Crisscross the poles at one end and tie securely. Sink the opposite ends into the ground, forming the frame for your tepee. At the base of each pole plant green beans. Train the bean plants up the poles. If you don't use any pesticides, the kids can snack while they play.

Summer Splash

Ah, summer! That time of year when schedules relax a bit. Remember how summer seemed to last forever when you were a child? Now it feels like it's over in a wink. I have made a conscious effort to enjoy those lazy days of summer. Do crafts outdoors where cleanup is a snap. Read under a shady tree, and don't forget the lemonade!

Summers around here can get very hot, so before our little ones could swim we needed to come up with ways for them to cool off. Soon we had the entire neighborhood joining in. Instead of water guns we use spray bottles that can be bought in the health and beauty section of most stores. The spray is much gentler than that of a water gun and they do not need to be filled quite so often.

Trike/Bike Wash

We all know how tempting it is to get soaked while washing the car, so we decided to let the kids wash their "vehicles." We gave each of them a bucket of water and a sponge and let them loose. It's so simple, but it kept them busy and cool for hours.

Sprinklers

Sprinklers are great fun for kids. They can run through them to their heart's content. If you don't have a lawn sprinkler, you can attach a nozzle to a hose, secure the hose to a pole, and let the fun happen. Our family likes to play musical sprinkler. The kids march around the sprinkler to music. When the music stops, the sprinkler goes on. Whoever gets wet sits out a turn.

Frozen Fruit

You can freeze many different kinds of fruit for a cool nutritious snack. Try bananas, strawberries, unseeded watermelon, cantaloupe, or honeydew.

AUTUMN FESTIVITIES

Autumn is the time to slow down after a busy summer. The days are getting shorter, and there are many wonderful harvest treats to enjoy. Take walks and enjoy the changing leaves with your children. Rake up the leaves, but don't forget to jump in the piles before you bag them. Visit an orchard and have your kids help you pick your own bushel of apples. Go to a pumpkin patch and let each child pick out their own pumpkin to carve.

Leaf Suncatchers

Materials: waxed paper, old crayons, crayon/pencil sharpener, leaves, iron and ironing board, newspaper.

Have the children gather colorful leaves. Look for ones that are not crumbled or bent. Give each child a piece of waxed paper. Have them arrange four to five leaves, depending on their size, on the paper. Sharpen the crayons and spread the shavings over the leaves. Place another piece of waxed paper on top. Place the newspaper on your ironing board to protect it. Put the layered waxed paper and leaves on top of the newspaper and cover with more newspaper. Quickly "iron" the waxed paper with a hot iron. When cooled, the layers will be fused together. Hang the suncatchers in a window for all to enjoy.

Roasting Chestnuts

Most people think of roasting chestnuts at Christmas, but they are less expensive and more available in the fall. To roast them, preheat your oven to 350. Slice an "x" in the shell of each nut. Place the nuts on a cookie tray and sprinkle them with water. Bake for 15 to 20 minutes or until the shells curl back. Test one by inserting a knife in to see if it is tender (much like a cake). Let the chestnuts cool but not get cold before enjoying. We like them best with a glass of cider.

Apple Cobbler

Apples are abundant in the fall and so delicious. Try this easier-than-pie recipe with your family.

Easy Apple Cobbler

1/4 cup butter
4 cups apples, peeled, cored, and sliced
1/2 cup sugar
1 tablespoon plus 2/3 cup baking mix (like Bisquick)
1/2 teaspoon cinnamon
2 tablespoons brown sugar
2 tablespoons milk

Preheat oven to 400°. In a casserole dish combine apples, sugar, 1 tablespoon baking mix, and cinnamon. In a medium bowl mix remain baking mix with brown sugar. Cut the butter into the dry ingredients until mix resembles coarse crumbs the size of small peas. (This will work better if the butter is chilled.) Stir in milk until moistened. Drop by spoonfuls onto apples. Bake for 30 minutes. Let stand for 5 minutes before eating. Add a scoop of vanilla ice cream to make it extra-yummy.

Make the Most out of Every Season

There once was a woman who claimed she loved every season. In the winter she would complain about the cold and yearn for spring. In the spring she was overwhelmed by spring cleaning and looked forward to summer. When summer came the heat exhausted her, and she longed for the cool breezes of fall. She loved every season, but she didn't enjoy any of them. Celebrate each season as it comes. Enjoy the moments you are given. Remember, with each passing season, your child is getting a little older—and so are you! You can't get these days back, so enjoy them, treasure them, love them.

Chapter 4

Milestone Celebrations

DURING THE PRESCHOOL YEARS children accomplish new skills daily. This is very exciting! Celebrate these accomplishments. Not only will the celebrations provide your child with rich memories to look back on, they will also help build your child's confidence and give him or her a sense of achievement. These are important traits to instill in your child now. Then, when it's time to send him to school or he meets up with the challenges life sends, he will lean on these shining moments in his past.

Celebrations don't have to be long and complicated. In our house they are often small, but they still make a huge difference in my children's attitudes toward trying new things. Libby, for example, always lets her big brother represent her in social situations. He would answer all questions and make all requests for her. If Mom and Dad weren't there, Nick would take care of things. When it was time for them to be split up in Sunday school, she fretted. I told her this was an important step in her life. I gave her a little pink pocketbook with a wallet containing her own homemade ID card, tissues, and a family photo. After this special presentation I explained that we thought she was a big girl now. Libby confidently walked into her Sunday school room the following week with her little pink purse perched on her shoulder just the way Mommy carries her bag. A few years later when she walked into her kindergarten class, that wallet and tissues had been transferred to her backpack.

Celebrate each step of your child's development so when she is an adult she will remember a full and happy childhood.

First Lost Tooth

The first tooth my son lost sent me to my room in tears. He wasn't a baby anymore; he was growing adult teeth. I carefully wrapped that tooth in plastic and taped it inside his baby book. For me it symbolized a new phase of his life.

We've been through all kinds of experiences with losing teeth. Nicholas lost his tooth in the middle of a museum. There's nothing like having your child sobbing while telling you he lost his tooth. At first I didn't understand what all the tears were about. It seemed the tooth had fallen out and been lost. Fortunately, after retracing our steps we did find the tiny white treasure.

Ice cream, Jell-O, pudding, and ice pops are excellent treats for celebrating lost teeth. They are soft and cold, which soothes sore mouths. We have been known to serve ice cream sundaes for dinner when one of our children loses a tooth. Eating dessert for a meal once in a while won't destroy their diet forever.

Some families have problems with fantasy characters like the Tooth Fairy and Santa. This is something for you to decide. Many families leave money under their child's pillow when the child loses a tooth; others leave new toothbrushes, special children's toothpaste, or a new cup for the child to rinse with when she brushes. All of these ideas promote good dental hygiene.

If you are going to let in the magic, really throw open the window. One family we know sprinkles glitter on the floor near their child's bed to reinforce the whimsy of the Tooth Fairy. Make a special Tooth

Fairy pillow with a pocket for the child's lost tooth. We use an empty film container, decorated with glow-in-the-dark paint for our children's lost teeth. It's a lot easier to find that container on their pillow in the dark than a tiny tooth. It's so much fun to crawl in your child's room and not be discovered. And it's a thrill to hear their amazed and delighted giggles when they discover your handiwork.

First Haircut

The first time a child goes for a "real" haircut can be a big event. Sitting in that big barber chair, covered with a huge apron, and being approached by a stranger with sharp scissors are the makings of a nightmare. However, if you surround that moment with the right preparation, you can turn it around into a celebration.

Take your child to the hairdresser with you so he can see what's going to happen. Practice having him sit still while you pretend to cut and style his hair. It is a big help to your child and the barber if your child knows how to behave.

My husband took advantage of going to the barbershop with our son by using it as a special "men only" trip. It's something they have done together every six weeks since Nick's first birthday. I must admit I did tag along the first time they went, to take pictures and save a piece of that soft baby hair for his baby book. Some hairdressers even provide special envelopes for baby's first haircut.

POTTY TRAINING

Potty training—just the thought can strike terror in a parent's mind. Fear not, all children do learn to use the bathroom eventually. Some take longer than others, but I've never heard of anyone in first grade wearing diapers. When this skill is mastered, it is definitely time for a celebration. Our family celebrated this milestone by taking a trip to Wal-Mart to pick out "big kid" underwear. We topped off the trip with some cookies at the snack shop. I know it doesn't sound like much, but the idea of a special shopping trip is all some children need to motivate them into succeeding in this area.

One mom I know bought plain training pants for her girls. They decorated these "big girl" pants with fabric paints. The girls thought their new underwear was so neat they were careful to keep them clean.

ABCs, 123s

Learning their ABCs and numbers are a preschooler's first academic achievements. You can use these ideas to either help them learn or to celebrate mastery of these skills. When we make these concepts fun, reading and mathematics will be more enjoyable in the later years. Remember, every experience your children have is a building block to their future.

Alphabet Walk

Go on a walk with your child and challenge her to find things that begin with each letter of the alphabet. Write one letter of the alphabet on each page of a small notepad. While you are walking, your child can mark off the letter pages when they spot something that begins with that letter. If you don't complete the entire alphabet, start where you stopped the next time you take a walk. This activity keeps little ones interested while you get some fresh air and exercise.

Easy Alphabet Soup

Any type of soup can easily be turned into alphabet soup. Look for a package of alphabet pasta on your next shopping trip. A handful of pasta added to the soup is enough to keep a preschooler happily munching and reciting her letters.

Letter Pancakes

Homemade pancakes are a favorite in our house. You can serve them for breakfast, lunch, or dinner. Pancakes are inexpensive, filling, and can be poured into any shape. For our ABC dinner I poured the batter into letter shapes. You can also pour it into numbers, using the same technique. It takes a quick hand and a little practice, but any mistakes quickly disappear. Plastic refillable ketchup or mustard squirt containers make pouring the letters even easier. Use prepackaged pancake mixes or make your own.

For approximately 16 pancakes you will need:

Flower Cookies

2 eggs
1 3/4 cups milk
1/4 cup oil
1 3/4 cups all-purpose flour
2 tablespoons sugar
4 teaspoons baking powder

Heat your griddle to medium-high heat (400°). When a few drops of water sprinkled on the griddle sizzle and bounce, the heat is just right. Beat eggs in a large bowl, then stir in milk and oil. Add remaining ingredients; stir just until large lumps disappear. For thicker pancakes add more flour, for thinner pancakes add more milk. Lightly grease heated griddle. Pour batter quickly into letter shapes on the griddle. Bake until bubbles form and edges start to dry. Turn and bake other side.

For some variety try adding one of the following to your batter:

1/2 cup shredded apples and 1/2 teaspoon of cinnamon
1 cup drained fresh or frozen blueberries (thawed and drained)
1/2 cup shredded cheese
1/2 cup bacon, cooked and crumbled
1/2 cup chopped nuts

Bread Shapes

My daughter loved shaping bread dough into letters and numbers when she was small. Children can use the letters to initial each place setting or spell out family members' names at mealtime. Use frozen bread dough for an easy, quick activity. If you have more time, and don't mind the mess, try creating dough from scratch. You'll have to provide some distraction for the little ones while the bread rises, but the squeals of delight when they get to punch down the risen dough is worth it.

Basic White Bread

For 2–3 dozen dough balls:

3 cups of flour plus 1 cup more
2 tablespoons dry milk
3 1/2 tablespoons sugar

2 teaspoons active dry yeast
3 tablespoons butter or margarine, melted
8 ounces of warm water (90°–100°, it should feel just warm to the touch)
1 1/2 teaspoons butter, softened, or 1 slightly beaten egg white

In a large bowl combine 3 cups of flour, dry milk, sugar, and yeast. In a small saucepan melt butter and mix with warm water. Add warm liquid to flour mix. Blend at low speed until moistened. By hand, stir in additional flour until dough pulls clear away from sides of bowl. On a floured surface, allow the children to knead the dough until smooth and elastic, about 5 minutes. Add more flour, if necessary, to achieve the correct consistency. Place dough in a greased bowl and cover with a cloth towel. Let the dough rise in a warm, draft-free place until doubled in size (approximately 1 hour).

Let the children punch down the dough several times to remove all air bubbles. Divide the dough into balls for each child. Allow them to shape letters with the dough. Place letters on greased cookie sheet. Cover with a cloth towel and allow to rise in warm place for about 30 to 35 minutes.

Preheat oven to 400°. Brush the letters with egg white or butter. Bake letters for 15 minutes or until golden brown.

Tablecloths

While you prepare a meal, your child can prepare the tablecloth. You will need paper large enough to cover the table (i.e., butcher paper, or tape several pieces of paper together), and crayons.

Cover the table with the paper. Set the table for the meal. Ask your preschooler to take the crayons and decorate the "tablecloth" with the letters that begin each item on the table. For example: by each plate a "p", by each cup a "c", etc. They can also make place cards for each family member using the first letter of their names.

Menus

Using construction paper and old magazines, help your little ones make menus for a meal by having them cut out photos of the food you will be serving and paste them in alphabetical order. When you give your children something to do while you prepare a meal, meal preparation is less harried. We have found that unoccupied children get into more trouble than busy ones.

It's fun to pick a letter and try to base a meal around foods that begin with that sound. A "b" meal may include some type of beef dish, broccoli, baked beans, and bread and butter. One of our favorites is "s": steak, shrimp, sweet potatoes, and squash. If this sounds like too much work, see if your child can pick out which dishes begin with a certain letter sound each evening. The "z" night might just tempt them to eat the zucchini. We have also used the letters in each child's name to plan a menu. Libby was lettuce salad, ice cream, broccoli, beef, and yams. Nicholas's meal consisted of noodles, iced cupcakes, carrots, ham, onions, lettuce, applesauce, and salad. We had great fun trying to find foods we liked and that complemented each other for these meals.

Remember, this isn't for every night, just for when you need to get out of a humdrum meal-planning mode or want to celebrate the mastery of a new skill.

Personal Letter Pizza

Most kids love pizza, and when they can make their own it's a fun craft too. We challenged our children to form their initials with the ingredients we used in making pizza. You can buy frozen pizza dough in your grocery store, or visit a local pizza shop (not a chain) to see if they will sell you the dough. You can also make your own dough at home.

Pizza Dough

For 2 thick crust personal letter pizzas
you will need:

1 1/2–2 cups all-purpose flour
1 teaspoon sugar

2 teaspoons active dry yeast
3/4 cup warm water
1 tablespoon cooking oil (olive oil tastes best, but vegetable oil works just as well)

In a large bowl combine 3/4 cup flour, sugar, and yeast. Mix in warm water and oil and blend until moistened. Stir in an additional 1/2 cup flour to form stiff dough. On a floured surface, have the children knead in 1/4 to 1/2 cup flour until dough is smooth and elastic. Place the dough in a greased bowl and cover loosely with a towel. Let the dough rise in a warm, draft-free place until light and doubled in size (30–45 minutes).

Preheat oven to 400°. Have the children punch down the dough several times to remove all air bubbles. Divide the dough into two balls and have the children press each half into a greased 6-inch pan. Spread each pizza with pizza sauce and cheese, then have the kids arrange the pizza toppings in the letter shapes of each child's name. Bake for 18–20 minutes. If your family prefers thin crust pizzas, divide the dough into four balls instead of two.

Try these topping suggestions: olives, pineapple, green peppers, ham, pepperoni, cooked and crumbled chopped meat, onions, or cooked and crumbled sausage.

New Baby

The arrival of a baby brother or sister in the family is cause for joy. It can also be a rough time for a preschooler who is used to being an only child. Include your child in the preparations and celebrations for this new life. When Libby was born, Nick was only fifteen months old. I was concerned that there would be sibling rivalry and jealousy. When I was pregnant, Jim and I were careful to refer to the baby as "our baby" or "Nicholas's baby." We tried to include Nick as much as possible in the coming event. We celebrated Nick's moving to a big boy bed several weeks before the baby's due date so he would not associate losing the crib to the new kid. My sister took Nick out shopping to pick out a gift for his new sister to welcome her home. She and her husband included him in the decorating of our front door with pink streamers and an "It's a Girl!" sign. Allowing him to feel like he was an important part of the arrival of this new family member made the transition from only child to big brother easier.

We were awaiting my daughter Sarah's arrival as I wrote this book. Nick and Libby helped me pack my bag and Sarah's. Libby loved picking out Sarah's homecoming outfit. We toured the hospital's maternity unit so they would know where I was going; I also brought them along when I had my ultrasound so they could see their new sister.

Shortly before the arrival of their second child, friends of ours allowed their three-year-old to help finish the baby's room. This big brother used his toy tools to check all the joints on the crib and the hinges on the door. His dad even had him test the smoke detector in the room. When the baby was born, this little guy took great pride in telling all visitors that he had made his sister's room safe.

Family Time Capsule

This fun craft makes a great gift from older siblings to the new baby. The real fun will come when the children are ten or fifteen years older and you open the time capsule to see what the family was like when the baby was born.

Let the kids decorate some large butcher paper and use it to wrap both top and bottom pieces of a shoe box. Have the children pick out the following items to include in your family time capsule: a current photo of each family member, a homemade card or drawing from each family member, and some special memento they would like the baby to have from them. You can also include a new-issue stamp from that year, a coin from that year, and the front page from a newspaper paper printed on the day the baby is born.

Each brother or sister who can't write yet can dictate to you what they think is important for the baby to know about your family and a "welcome to the family" message.

Birth Announcements

Get your children involved in making an original birth announcement for them to send to family and friends. If you have supplies handy, the children can do this project while you and baby are in the hospital. It will help your caregiver if you provide something for your children to do that is connected with this big event. On white construction paper have your children draw a picture of the whole new family or just a picture of the new baby and them. On another paper print the important information:

Name:
Date of Birth:
Weight:
Length:
Parents:
Big Sister and/or Big Brother:

Take the sheets to a copy shop and have them printed back-to-back on pink or blue paper (or mint green or purple or whatever colors the big sister or brother prefers). Now they are ready for the proud older siblings to hand out to friends and family.

Other Pivotal Moments to Celebrate

There are so many accomplishments in a preschooler's life that you could hold weekly celebrations. We held a "company meal" just for our family when our children began to learn good table manners. The meal was always something simple, but we would serve it with a tablecloth, candles, and our good dishes. Everyone dressed for the meal in his or her Sunday clothes, and we played classical music in the background. Nicholas and Libby enjoyed it so much it has become a much-repeated tradition.

It's so important to recognize small moments, like when a child remembers to take care of something, or does a good job sharing, or is polite and considerate to an adult. Don't let these moments go unnoticed if you want the obedient behavior to continue. All that may be needed is a big hug and a word of appreciation, but I have also on occasion created a medal or diploma to honor the mastery of a new skill. Another idea is to send your child a note through the mail to tell him how proud you are of him. Getting mail addressed to them is a real thrill to a child.

We are so used to correcting unwanted behavior that we sometimes forget to acknowledge when our children get it right. My mother always used to tell me, "You can get more with honey than you do with vinegar." Our children love us and want to please us. Let them know when they do.

CHAPTER 5

Getting Family and Friends into the Act

WE LOVE SHARING GOOD TIMES with friends and family. It's important for your children to have connections with people outside of their household. Family and friends are wonderful gifts you can share. Each person you introduce into your child's world brings experiences and lessons you cannot provide. In addition, adult relatives and friends support your parenting, and other children help your little ones develop social skills like sharing, independence, and self-confidence. Encourage these relationships by providing special times for your family to get together with others. We also try to plan activities that cultivate long-distance relationships with family members who live in other states.

Finding Out about Family

Helping your children learn about their family history will give them a sense of belonging. We all love to hear about the time Grandma met Grandpa and the family tree took root. We also love to hear our immediate family's history. My children love to go over their own "stories." Every birthday we sit down with their baby book and tell the story of how they came to be a part of our family. It reminds them of just how special they are.

Photos and Stories

We live at least a state away from most of our family and don't get to see them as often as we would like. It is important to me that my children know their family despite the distance. On one wall in our home we have framed photos of many family members so our children will be accustomed to their faces. We also share our experiences and memories of these special people with our children so that Nick and Libby feel as if they know their relatives. That way, when we get together they don't spend time being shy but already feel a comfortable familiarity with their relatives.

Mini Family Photo Albums

You could also make individual family books for each child. Photo developers often provide small "brag books" when you get your film developed. If yours doesn't, you can purchase them inexpensively. Cover photos of family members with clear contact paper before you place them in the mini photo albums so they will not be damaged if accidentally removed. Now your child can have their very own family photo album to look at whenever they choose.

Pull out your old photo albums and use them as storybooks. I think Nicholas and Libby are the only people in the world who love looking at pictures of me in elementary and high school. They especially enjoy hearing stories about when I was their age and the times I went on a Girl Scout camping trip and performed in the high school play. When Nick started learning to ride a bicycle, he asked for a story about when I learned to ride my bicycle. I found a picture of myself on my first bicycle and told them about my own experience. The more details I could include, the better the story. It's fun to have such an appreciative audience for the pictures and stories the rest of my family have seen and heard a thousand times!

Ethnic Food and Fun

Our family has many ethnic origins, and that means a variety of taste treats and fun traditions.

What are your ethnic origins? It's educational and fun to set aside an evening to sample the flavors from the countries of your ancestors.

Our background is Italian, Irish, and German, which gives us much to choose from. It's fun to invite over family or friends who share the same nationality and sample different foods. Keep in mind I said "sample." Don't expect your child to make a complete meal out of a new food. It's an accomplishment if your child learns to try a little of something new.

To make the meal even more special, play background music that matches your theme. Go to the library and find stories and games that originated from the culture you are celebrating. While the meal is cooking, you can have your children make their own version of the flag of that nation. You can fill an hour or a day, depending on what you find.

Grandparents and Extended Family

Grandparents and other older adults are a rich resource for you and your children. They provide a view of life seasoned with experience. If your children are not blessed to have living grandparents, tell your children about your experiences with these people. Share photos and mementos of them so your children will have a connection to the people in their family who contributed so much to who you are. My dad passed away when Libby was five years old. Nick and Libby never got to have a relationship with him because his last years were spent with Alzheimer's disease in a nursing home. I have made sure they know him through me. There is so much of my dad that I see in my children. I let them know that Libby's love of drawing and Nick's interest in electronics and coin collecting are things they shared with their grandpa. It gives them a vital connection to my family and their heritage.

I also look for other older adults to fill the grandparent role for my children. It's so important for children to have multigenerational relationships. Find interests your children can share with their grandparents and other older adults, and provide the necessary supplies, opportunities, and education for your children to develop these interests.

My Uncle Ben is a retired architect who now uses his time to paint beautiful landscapes. Libby is quite the art lover. This was a great relationship in the making. I took Libby to the library and borrowed some wonderful art books. We purchased some paints and materials for her for a birthday gift. Now when we visit Uncle Ben, they have so much to discuss and share. They paint side by side in his basement-turned-art-studio. She looks forward to their visits, and I can only imagine the sage wisdom being passed from generation to generation while the paint hits the canvas.

Audio Recordings

Children love to hear about Grandma's life as much as Grandma loves to hear about her grandchildren. Encourage grandparents to record their family stories and favorite storybooks for your children to enjoy when they are apart. Tape recorders and blank tapes are wonderful gifts to give both children and grandparents. Children can record their "letters" to Grandpa—and vice versa! Grandpa not only gets the news but the sound effects as well.

Artwork

Children produce more artwork than any parent knows what to do with. We feel guilty throwing it away, but we simply can't keep it all. What to do? Use the back side of those finger-painted pictures and crayon drawings as stationery. What a treat it is to get something in the mail that is not a bill! Phone calls may be quick and easy, but what are you left with? Letters can be reread and savored. If you don't want to write on the artwork, at least remember to share some of those precious masterpieces with those who love your children. Stick one in the envelope each time you write a letter to a relative. It will truly be appreciated, and when your child visits Aunt Mary's house and sees their artwork on the refrigerator, they will feel so special.

FRIENDSHIP TEA

Most everyone can remember the house in the neighborhood where the children always gathered—it was a place where a mom with a childlike heart lived. She didn't mind the noise or clutter as long as she could help her children develop their creativity and relationships with others. When I was expecting, I decided I wanted my house to be the neighborhood gathering place. What I didn't realize at that time was how much effort it would take! It challenges my creativity and patience. I learned to scale down and provide manageable but memorable play dates for my children. I also discovered what types of activities children love to do again and again.

Little girls (and big ones too) love tea parties. I found if Libby had one girlfriend over to visit, a tea party for a snack or lunch was the perfect event. It's so popular it's worth investing in some props. Older girls really feel special when you provide real china. (When your daughter is quite small, two to three years old, you will probably want to use a plastic play tea set.) Libby and I visited garage sales to purchase pretty cups, saucers, a creamer, a sugar bowl, and even a teapot. If you are nervous about the girls breaking things and getting cut, Corelle dishes are unbreakable but still "grown-up." We purchased only enough dishes for two girls. Teas seem to work best with two rather than a crowd.

The first time Libby's friend Liza came to visit I was baking muffins, and Libby asked if they could have a tea party. When I said I would call them when it was ready, they happily skipped up to Libby's room. When they reappeared minutes later, I noticed that they had rummaged through our costume box and dressed for the occasion. No one had to tell them how to have a tea party or how to make it an event—it came naturally. I got out the teacups, brewed some decaffeinated tea in a teapot, and set the table for my guests. Muffins, some grapes, and small cream cheese and jelly sandwiches rounded out the meal. The girls used their very best manners and were occupied for an hour or more.

Here are some delicious treats for you to try at your next tea.

Chocolate Chip Muffins

This is by far the most requested snack in our house.

For 12 muffins you will need:

2 cups flour

1/2 cup sugar
3 teaspoons baking powder
1/2 cup chocolate chips
3/4 cup milk
1/3 cup oil
1 egg

Preheat the oven to 400°. Grease 12 muffin cups, or line with paper baking cups. Mix flour, sugar, baking powder, and chocolate chips in a large bowl. Make a well in the middle of the dry ingredients and add the milk, oil, and egg all at once. Stir until dry ingredients are moistened. Fill prepared muffin cups 2/3 full. Bake for 15 minutes or until light golden brown. Cool 1 minute before removing from pan.

Vanilla or Almond Milk

If you are uncomfortable serving tea to little ones, try a flavored milk.
For each cup you will need:

1 cup milk
1 teaspoon of sugar
1/4 teaspoon vanilla or almond flavoring

Gently warm milk in a saucepan or microwave to take the chill off. Stir in sugar and flavoring. Enjoy!

Favorite Tea Sandwiches

Tea sandwiches are thin and delicate. For each sandwich, remove the crust from two slices of bread. Flatten the bread slightly with a rolling pin. Spread a thin layer of your favorite sandwich fixings and cut into interesting shapes using cookie cutters. Cream cheese and jelly, peanut butter, egg salad, tuna salad, and lettuce and tomato are the most popular items on our tea menu.

More Tea Activities

You can use the tea theme to plan an entire morning of activities that culminates in the actual tea. The girls can make place mats, place cards, and a centerpiece for the table, and they can decorate hats to wear.

For the place mats and place cards provide the girls with construction paper, stamps, crayons, scraps of material, lace, glue, and stickers. For the centerpiece make available some artificial flowers (or real flowers if your garden can provide them), a container, and some lace and ribbons. You can find play hats at garage sales, thrift stores, or craft stores. Supply glue, flowers, lace, ribbons, and perhaps some beads or gems. The girls bring their imaginations. It's fun to see what they will create on their own.

You can use the preparation for the tea to teach the girls how to set a table. You may even want to include them in snack preparation. Any of these activities can be as elaborate or as simple as you choose to make them.

Being a Good Neighbor

It's important for children to understand that they are part of a community. I try to plan activities that teach my children about their community, the people who live and work in it, and their responsibility to those people. A simple walk around the block is the beginning of this education. It's also good for them to know how to get around their town or neighborhood and who is safe to talk to if they get lost.

Who Works Here?

When you run your errands to the bank, post office, grocery, service station, or cleaners, explain to your child the kinds of work these people do and why we need them. Look for simple ways for you and your children to show these people how much you appreciate their services.

Our children love our postal carrier. "Aunt Lucy" will often find a note from them to her in our mailbox when she stops by. When it's cold and snowy, we've been known to leave some cookies and a thermos of hot cocoa for her. We appreciate how she helps to keep our community running smoothly.

Secret Angels

It's fun to do good deeds in secret or just unexpectedly for your neighbors. Think of simple acts you and your children can do for the people who live closest to you. Raking leaves, sending cards, and leaving treats and flowers are all within the abilities of a preschooler.

Friendship Fudge

This fudge recipe is so simple a preschooler can help. It's also so yummy that your neighbors, postal carrier, oilman, or whoever is the lucky recipient will love you for it.

The best part is that one batch of fudge goes a long way, so there will be plenty for the gift givers to enjoy too!

Friendship Fudge

For 1 batch of fudge you will need:

2 pounds powdered sugar
1 cup unsweetened cocoa
1 cup butter or margarine
1/2 cup milk
2 teaspoons vanilla

Have the children mix the powdered sugar and cocoa in a large microwave-safe bowl. Without stirring, add milk and butter. Microwave on high until butter is melted (5 minutes). Add vanilla and stir until smooth. Help the children spread the mixture into a greased baking pan. Chill until firm (we usually leave it in the refrigerator overnight). Cut into small pieces and wrap. Place in little boxes, baskets, or just paper plates covered with pretty paper.

TALENT SHOWS

Most preschoolers are natural performers. They are completely uninhibited. They hear music in a store and begin to bop and dance. Why not provide an opportunity for them to entertain each other? Invite over some of your child's friends, provide music, dress-up costumes, and some preschool instruments, and the show will take care of itself.

Easy Instruments

The simplest instruments are pots and pans for drums and funnels for horns, but if you want to provide more activities, let your budding musicians make their own noisemakers.

For an original band you will need to collect funnels, ribbons, streamers, empty toilet paper or paper towel rolls, several empty plastic bottles, foil or tin pie plates, empty oatmeal boxes, unsharpened pencils, shoe boxes, rubber bands, large beans, rice, glue, colorful paper, tape, crayons, markers, yarn, and buttons.

Tambourine

An adult should punch 6 holes around the edge of the pie plate. Have a child thread a piece of yarn through a button. Put the piece of yarn through a hole in the pie plate, knotting tightly to hold the button in place. Continue threading yarn with buttons and placing them in holes around the plate. Allow enough slack in the yarn so the button can freely hit the pie plate when it is shaken. Give it a good shake, and you're in the band!

Drum

Have your child draw with markers or crayons on a piece of paper. Use the paper to wrap an oatmeal box. Make sure the paper is securely glued or taped. A new, unsharpened pencil makes a great drumstick or the child can use his hand like a tom-tom to keep time.

Horn

Decorate a toilet paper or paper towel roll with crayons or markers. Hang ribbons or streamers from one end. You can't get much simpler than this. Playing this horn comes naturally to most children.

Maracas

Remove the labels from empty plastic drink bottles. Have your child use a funnel to pour 1/4 to 1/2 cup of beans or rice into each bottle. Put glue around the rim of the bottle opening and twist closed securely. The beans will produce a different, heavier sound than that of the rice.

Guitar or Harp

Have your child decorate shoe boxes with markers or crayons. With the lid removed, stretch rubber bands over the boxes. Cut an oval hole in the lid of the shoe box and tape securely in place. Children can "strum" their guitar through the oval on the top of the shoe box.

Story Acting

Nicholas has always loved to act things out. We would read a story, and he would perform it. Invite your children and their friends to be the actors for a favorite story while you are the narrator. Try to find a story they know and love and that has consistent characters. It also needs to be relatively short. Nursery rhymes and Aesop's fables work well. Nicholas and Libby particularly like acting out *The Tortoise and the Hare* in our backyard.

Relationships Make Life Memorable

Strong relationships and the ability to nurture and develop them are one of the most valuable gifts we can pass on to our children. Sometimes inviting over another family or even my own family seems like the last thing I want to tackle. The wonderful thing is that, whenever I do, we all enjoy our time together so very much. I need to remind myself that relationships are what make life memorable. I remember the things people have taught me and the time they spent listening to me, not whether or not their house was spotless or what meal we had. Don't get caught up in the details of planning events; spontaneity makes for the best times. Reach out to those whom God has placed around you. They, and your family, will be so glad you did.

Silly Stuff

WE'VE ALL HAD THOSE DAYS when nothing is going the way we planned. The kids are cranky and uncooperative. Appliances are not working correctly. The weather is terrible. The general mood of your home is *blah!* That's the time to drop everything and get silly. The ideas in this chapter have saved my sanity on more than a few occasions. Sometimes we need to stop trying to swim upstream and instead enjoy the view floating down the river.

RAINY DAY CELEBRATION

Rainy or cold days are wonderful opportunities for fun, cozy times. They can also be days when children and moms get a bit stir-crazy. Here are some atmosphere-changing ideas for both inside and outside.

Indoor Picnic

Pack a picnic lunch, and take a walk around the house looking for the perfect picnic spot. Spread an old tablecloth or blanket on the floor and enjoy your snack. Help your children imagine they are in the park or at the lake. Describe what you might be seeing or doing if you were there.

Animal Safari

Hide your preschooler's stuffed animals around the house: under beds, peeking around furniture, inside closets and cabinets you don't mind your kids getting into. Sit with them and describe a jungle filled with wild animals. Turn off all the lights, and let them use a flashlight to go on a safari to "capture" all the animals.

Crazy Maze

Children love to crawl through and around things. Create a maze through your house using furniture, laundry baskets, furniture cushions, pillows, and stuffed toys. You can even use empty boxes to create tunnels for your maze. See if your children can crawl through the maze in a specific length of time.

Camping in the Great Indoors

On rainy days my children love indoor camping. We started by making tents using blankets draped over several chairs or a table. The next rainy day we tried using rope tied to doorknobs on opposite walls and draped a sheet over the rope. Any of these designs work; the idea is just to give them a cozy, private place. You can put cereal in a small paper bag for a "campfire snack." Don't forget to provide a flashlight. Libby loves setting up house with her pillows, blankets, dolls, and books.

Indoor S'mores

The best camping snack is s'mores, and you can make them for your children without the campfire.

Indoor S'mores

For each s'more you will need:

- 2 graham crackers
- 1 marshmallow
- 1 small piece of chocolate

Top one cracker with chocolate and a marshmallow. Place it on a paper towel and microwave on high for 10 seconds or until you see the marshmallow puff up. Cover with the second cracker and lightly press together. You can also make another version using the same instructions but substituting chocolate graham crackers and skipping the chocolate.

Outside the House

Rainy days are our favorite days to visit our local library. Take advantage of a cozy nook in the children's section after you choose something for yourself from the adult bookshelves or magazines. Our library offers a bank of computers with children's programs and a daily story hour. Check out what your library offers.

When it is not too cold we love to walk in the rain. Just because it's wet outside doesn't mean you should stay in all day. Get each family member (including yourself) a bright rain slicker and some boots, and experience the joy of splashing in the puddles. Getting out for even fifteen to thirty minutes can change your mood.

Backward Day

After one particularly hectic day, I told Nick and Libby that the next day I was going to do everything backward and hoped that it would turn out better than today. The next morning I was greeted with a surprise. The kids took me seriously. Nick came down with all his clothes on backward. Libby wanted to know, since it was backward day, what was for dinner instead of breakfast. Their enthusiasm prompted me to throw caution to the wind and join in the fun. We ate dinner for breakfast, wore clothes backward, brushed our teeth before eating, ate dessert first, and played before chores. It was great fun and gave me a reason to explain why we do things in the order we do.

Color Day

Have you ever noticed what an effect color can have on a person's mood? There are cheerful colors, comforting colors, and calming colors. Why not plan a day around a color to help set the mood of your family? Reds or yellows are a great pick-me-up on a dreary day. Challenge the children to go through their clothes and dress in the designated color. On a red day they can draw pictures of things that are red. Lunch can be macaroni and meatballs with tomato sauce, or tomato soup. Serve cranberry or cherry punch. Top it off with strawberry Jell-O for dessert. Use red construction paper for place mats. It doesn't matter what color you use; adding color to the day will brighten the frame of mind of your whole family.

Rainbow Scavenger Hunt

Kids love scavenger hunts. The idea of trying to discover something before anyone else is quite a thrill. This simple color scavenger hunt works well for preschoolers.

Assign each child a color, and ask him or her to find five to ten items that have that color on the them. Another approach is to give your child slips of paper of each color of the rainbow. They need to find something that matches each slip of paper and place it in a laundry basket. Scavenger hunts are great for moms because they can take from ten minutes to half an hour. Lollipops of all colors are great rewards for the hunters when the game is done.

Art Show

Most children love creating things. They enjoy coloring, painting, drawing, using stamps, cutting and pasting, playing with play dough, and building with blocks. They also love getting some attention for their efforts. Libby is famous for leaving little pieces of her artwork all over the house for Jim and me to find. She gets so hurt when we fail to acknowledge her gifts. It's worse if she discovers we have dared to throw some of it out.

It is totally unrealistic to keep every little scrap of paper she leaves for us, and there was only so much we could send to Grandma and the aunts and uncles, so I decided we would hold an art show. We displayed her handiwork and allowed her to decide which were the best. Those pieces became a part of her "blue ribbon" collection. The blue ribbon collection is stored in a box in the attic for her. The art show idea was a hit and prompted Nick to pursue some creative activities of his own. We even took photos of his building block creations to add to the exhibits.

Art Display Ideas

- To create an easy dinnertime art exhibit, spread your child's pictures on the table and cover with a clear plastic tablecloth. Set the table for dinner as usual. While the family is enjoying their meal, the children can talk about each picture.
- If you have an outdoor clothesline, you can create an open-air gallery. Clothespin your child's paper to the line. Family and friends can stroll through the rows of artwork and enjoy.
- One family I know has a revolving art display on their refrigerator. Purchase some inexpensive, light picture frames and a strip of magnetic tape (available at craft stores). Letter each child's name on one frame and let them decorate them. Display children's artwork in their frame on the refrigerator door. Each week have them choose their favorite new piece and replace the previous week's selection.
- Photograph all your child's artwork and keep the photos together in a special art photo album. This is a great idea for those with limited space, and your child will have this keepsake for years to come.

Pet Birthday

We have no idea when the birthday of our dog, Clara, is because we adopted her through a shelter. Libby, who is fond of celebrating birthdays, thought we should not deprive our dog of a party. I picked a day in March because that is usually the month when we are all getting a bit stir-crazy and need an event.

We serve special treats, play some games, and have cake. The dog gets cards, wrapped dog biscuits, and lots of attention. Here are some pet-themed foods to get you started:

Puppy Chow (for People)

The first time I tried this was at a church potluck supper. Children and adults loved it.

For one batch you will need:

- 1 cup chocolate chips
- 1 cup peanut butter (smooth)
- 1/4 pound butter or margarine
- 8 cups Chex cereal
- 2 cups powdered sugar

In a large microwave-safe bowl melt the chocolate chips, peanut butter, and butter together in a microwave for about 2 minutes. Mix in cereal, coating well. Place the mixture in a paper grocery sack and add powdered sugar. Shake well to coat and serve.

Kitty Lunch

You can make cute edible "mice" to celebrate a cat's special day.

For each mouse you will need:

half of a hard roll
tuna salad
almond slices
M&M candies
licorice laces

Hollow out half of a hard roll and fill it with tuna salad. Use the almond slices for mouse ears, M&Ms for the eyes and nose, and licorice for whiskers and a tail. When having your pet's celebration, if you are feeling really silly, let the children lap their milk out of shallow bowls.

Circus

I certainly could not leave out some of the fun things we've tried that the circus has conjured up. The circus is a magical, sparkly, exotic place and children love to imitate it. That's why the circus has been so popular for over two hundred years.

Pull out the face paint and costume box. Let each child decide what circus role they would like to play. The ringmaster can sport a handlebar mustache; there are also tigers, lions, bears, acrobats, and, of course, clowns. Getting your kids suited up can take a while. Let them enjoy the activity for as long as they seem interested.

Girls love to create headbands or hats to look like trapeze artists. Provide them with lots of feathers, beads, and stones to glue onto bands of construction paper, then staple the construction paper in a circle that fits around their heads like a crown.

When the children are dressed in their finery, put on some lively music and have a costume parade around the house or yard. When the parade is over, don't forget to serve lemonade and popcorn or animal crackers.

Put together your own version of a circus. Children can portray animals, do some silly tumbling, and walk an imaginary high wire. Take the time to sit and watch their show. The ten minutes or so it takes to give the children this attention (don't forget lots of applause) helps to build their confidence.

Western Roundup

Little boys are fascinated with the Old West. They love dressing up in hats and vests and pretending they are riding the range. On a difficult day, why not use this interest to your advantage? I have found that if I read a story to my little ones and provide some props, their imagination keeps them busy. Read about Pecos

Bill and other Wild West legends as well as books about famous Americans who opened up the West, like Daniel Boone and Davy Crockett. Your librarian could probably help you find children's literature on any theme that interests you. Try to stick to classics and biographies. By doing this you are building your children's knowledge of history and literature.

Cowboy Grub

Serve cut-up hot dogs with beans in an aluminum pie plate with a piece of buttered bread. The children can sit in a circle on the ground to eat, just like the cowpokes did out on the range.

Campfire Sing-Along

You don't need a real campfire to have a sing-along. You can share campfire songs with your children. If you don't know any "cowboy" songs, teach your children some patriotic favorites like "This Land Is My Land" or "America the Beautiful." Nicholas's favorite is "Happy Trails to You." Children love to sing, and listening to their little voices is a joy to any parent. It's fun to tape-record them singing and play it back another time.

Cars and Trains

When Nick and Libby were little, I quickly noticed a basic difference between boys and girls.

Libby gave every toy a personality and relationship to every other toy. Whether it was dolls or balls, there were a mommy and a daddy and children. Nick, on the other hand, gave everything a motor with a noise. Every toy, whether a vehicle or a stuffed animal, became motorized. It was a very interesting observation. Instead of fighting his fascination with the mechanical, I created ways to build on it.

Create a Vehicle

Occasionally bring home a cardboard box from the grocer's. Encourage your preschooler to design his or her own car or train. Fold the top of the box in so your child can safely sit in the box. Provide crayons, colored paper, and glue to decorate the car. Paper plates or pie tins make excellent wheels and a steering wheel.

When the vehicle is finished, provide some old maps and ask where they are going. Have them "map" out their route. Give them a kiss and a snack for their trip, and tell them you'll see them when they get back from their imaginary journey. Children love it when adults join in their pretend world.

BIRD-WATCHING

I have found birdfeeders to be a wonderful way to occupy my children's attention during the long winter months. We placed two feeders outside the kitchen window so Nicholas and Libby could watch the antics of our feathered friends from the warmth of the house. They enjoyed bird-watching so much I purchased a bird identification book, and they keep track of every new bird they discover at our "birdie snack bar."

One morning was particularly busy at our feeders, so we declared it a bird celebration. For lunch I made spaghetti and meatballs and arranged them to look like a nest with eggs.

If you wanted to extend this theme, you could purchase supplies at a local craft store and let each child decorate his or her own birdhouse. Activities that encourage children to study wildlife, even in a suburban backyard, encourage them to have a greater awareness of the wonderful world God has created.

Help Your Children Develop Their Creativity

I know many parents who find it easier to purchase a toy for their child than deal with the mess of creating a plaything. Resist this urge. Children need to go through the process of creation. When they use their imaginations to build a car or a tent, they are learning. It helps develop their decision-making ability. It builds their confidence and self-esteem. It gives them practice in solving problems. These are all vital traits they will need to succeed as adults. When parents allow their children to develop their creativity, they are investing in their future. Isn't that worth the mess?

Chapter 7

Planned Attacks on Boredom

DID YOU EVER NOTICE that the anticipation prior to an event can be as much fun as the event itself? It's amazing the power a red circle on the calendar can have to motivate us and give us something to look forward to.

I need to plan activities into our calendar to help keep me from getting stale. As moms, we can have fun learning new historical facts and sharing them with our families. The suggestions in this chapter work best if you can plan them for the dates indicated. At the beginning of a month, try to pick two or three to work into your schedule. Don't try to do them all in one year, or the novelty will wear off. But let me warn you, any idea you try may be so popular you will be forced to repeat it for years to come.

I find ideas like these on calendars, in encyclopedias, or at the library. You can hunt for some original ones to add to the list. The main idea is to keep the activity simple. I have tried not to include the popular holidays and events. Sometimes it's more fun to celebrate the somewhat obscure.

January

January is a month I need to have some special things planned. There are no real holidays to look forward to and the excitement of Christmas is waning.

January 8—Singer Elvis Presley's Birthday (1935)

Play some of Elvis' greatest hits while you bop around doing the housecleaning.

January 9—First U.S. Balloon Flight (1793)

Buy a helium balloon and see if the kids can get it to float from room to room without touching it with their hands.

January 11—International Thank You Day

Help the kids make thank-you notes for those special people in your life. Perhaps you still need to write thank-you notes for those Christmas gifts you received from out-of-town relatives. Take a trip to the post office to mail them.

January 18—Author A. A. Milne's Birthday (1882)

Read *Winnie the Pooh and the Blustery Day* while you snack on biscuits and honey. (Do not serve honey to a child under age two.)

January 22—National Popcorn Day

Popcorn Toppings

Sprinkle some new toppings (Parmesan cheese or your favorite spice) on a big bowl of popcorn. Melt cheddar cheese on freshly popped popcorn by spreading your popcorn on a baking sheet. Heat your oven to 250°. Grate 1/2 cup cheddar cheese on the popcorn and put it into the oven for 5 to 7 minutes. It's gooey but good.

Microwave Caramel Popcorn

For six cups of caramel popcorn you will need:

6 cups of popped popcorn
1/2 cup almonds (optional)
1/4 cup brown sugar, firmly packed
2 tablespoons light corn syrup
1/2 cup margarine or butter

1/4 teaspoon baking soda
1/8 teaspoon salt

Combine popcorn and almonds in a large microwave-safe bowl. In another, 4-cup microwave-safe bowl combine brown sugar, corn syrup, margarine or butter, and salt.

Microwave on high for 2 minutes and stir. Microwave on high an additional 2 to 3 minutes or until mixture comes to a rolling boil. Stir in baking soda. Pour over popcorn and almonds. Mix well to coat. Microwave the popcorn mix on high for 2 minutes. Spread on waxed paper to cool. Enjoy!

Popcorn Balls

You will need one batch of microwave caramel popcorn to make about a dozen popcorn balls. While the microwave caramel popcorn is still warm, use buttered hands to quickly and firmly press mix into balls. Wrap each ball in plastic wrap and share these portable treats with neighbors and friends.

January 24—Gold Discovered in California (1848)

Put some water, pennies, and sand in a dish basin. Give the children kitchen strainers and let them pan for shiny pennies. You can clean pennies so they really shine by soaking them in a mixture of baking soda and vinegar. The kids should get a kick out of seeing the baking soda and vinegar erupt.

January 26—Australia Day (1788)

Invite your children to pretend they are kangaroos and try shrimp on the "barbie" for dinner.

Shrimp on the Barbie

For four servings you will need:

- 1 lb. large raw shrimp, shelled and deveined
- 4 slices lime (optional)
- 1 each, red and yellow bell pepper, seeded and cut to one-inch chunks
- 1/2 cup prepared smoky-flavor barbecue sauce
- 2 tablespoons Worcestershire sauce
- 2 tablespoons cayenne pepper sauce
- 1 clove garlic, minced

Thread shrimp, peppers, and lime alternately onto metal skewers. Combine barbecue sauce, Worcestershire sauce, pepper sauce, and garlic in a small bowl. Mix well. Brush mixture on skewers.

Place skewers on barbecue grill, reserving sauce mixture. Grill over hot coals for 15 minutes or until the shrimp turns pink. Turn and baste often with reserved sauce. Do not baste during the last 5 minutes of cooking. Remove the shrimp, lime, and peppers from the skewers and serve with rice.

February

February is the shortest month of the year, but it is packed with interesting events to explore. The most popular commemorative days are Ground Hog Day, St. Valentine's Day, Martin Luther King Day, and Presidents' Day. It is also Black History and Dental Health month.

February 4—Aviator Charles Lindbergh's Birthday (1902)

Visit the airport. Watch the planes take off and land.

February 7—Author Laura Ingalls Wilder's Birthday (1867)

Celebrate pioneer life. Read some of *Little House in the Big Woods*, the first of Laura Ingalls Wilder's wonderful books. Enjoy some cornbread with homemade butter.

Cornbread

For nine servings you will need:

1 cup all-purpose flour
1 cup cornmeal
2 tablespoons sugar
4 teaspoons baking powder

1 cup milk
1 egg, slightly beaten
1/4 cup cooking oil or melted shortening

Preheat the oven to 425°. In a bowl, combine flour, cornmeal, sugar, and baking powder. Stir in milk, oil, and egg. Beat by hand until smooth. Pour batter into greased eight- or nine-inch square pan. Bake for 18 to 22 minutes or until toothpick inserted comes out clean.

Homemade Butter

1 small jar with a lid (a baby food jar is ideal)
1/2 cup heavy whipping cream

Pour the cream into the jar, leaving space at the top. Close the lid securely. Have your child hold the jar tightly in both hands and shake. Keep shaking until chunks of butter form. If your child gets tired, have him or her pass the jar to someone else to take a turn shaking. When chunks of butter form, spoon them into a bowl and add a few sprinkles of salt, if you wish. Spread the butter on warm cornbread.

You can also make butter using a hand mixer. My dad and I accidentally discovered this while we were trying to make whipped cream for a cake. We whipped it too long and discovered sweet butter.

February 9—U.S. Weather Bureau Began Operations (1870)

Discuss the weather with your child. What is weather, and how does it affect us? Buy an inexpensive outdoor thermometer. Help children come up with their own weather report. Listen to the weather report on the radio and see how accurate it is.

February 11—National Inventors' Day; Thomas Edison's Birthday (1847)

Point out some of the things we use in our homes that Thomas Edison helped to create. Invite children to invent something of their own. Provide paper and pencils for them to sketch it out. Use play dough, straws, popsicle sticks, and whatever items you can provide to help them build a model of their invention.

February 26—Buffalo Bill Cody's Birthday (1846)

Help your children make cowboy vests complete with fringes out of paper grocery bags. For each vest you will need: 1 paper grocery bag, scissors, crayons, construction paper, glue.

Cut the paper grocery bag up the middle for the opening of the vest. In the bottom of the bag cut a hole for your child's neck. Cut armholes in the sides of the bag. Turn the vest inside out so the plain inside of the bag is showing. Have your children decorate their vests as colorfully as they can using the crayons, colored paper, and glue.

March

In our part of the country March is a windy, blustery month that is completely unpredictable as far as weather is concerned. We enjoy getting outside again, flying kites and looking for the first migratory birds. March is the month Canadian geese, snow geese, and tundra swans are on the move. But the winter is not over yet, so I try to keep some fresh indoor activities on hand for those last-of-the-year snow days.

March 2—Author Dr. Seuss' Birthday (1904)

Wear silly hats while reading your favorite Dr. Seuss books. Add green food coloring to scrambled eggs and enjoy them with fried ham.

March 3—Inventor Alexander Graham Bell's Birthday (1847)

Paper Cup Telephone

Make a telephone using string and two paper cups. Punch a hole in the bottom of the cups. Thread one end of the string through the bottom of each cup and secure it with a knot. Stretch the string out and pull securely. Talk to your child over the "wire."

Telephone Game

Have your children line up in a row. Whisper a silly message or rhyme to the first child in line. Have the children pass the message down the line by whispering in the next child's ear. How has the message changed by the time the last child received it? Talk about giving clear messages.

March 8—Author Kenneth Grahame's Birthday (1859)

Find a cozy spot and enjoy Kenneth Grahame's wonderful stories in *The Wind and the Willows.*

March 11—Johnny Appleseed Day

Share the American folktale of Johnny Appleseed. Wear pots for hats. Enjoy applesauce, caramel apples, or apple pie for a snack.

Applesauce

For six servings you will need:

6 to 8 apples, peeled, cored, and cubed
1/2 cup sugar
1 teaspoon cinnamon (optional)

In a large saucepan simmer the apples over low heat for 15 to 20 minutes or until soft. Remove from heat. Add sugar and cinnamon. Mix well. Using a fork or potato masher, mash apple mix. Let cool.

Caramel Apples

For easy-to-make caramel apples, purchase some caramel sauce used for ice cream sundaes. Core and slice apples. Heat the caramel sauce in a small bowl in the microwave according to package direction. Allow the children to dip their apple slices into the caramel.

March 12—U.S. Post Office Established (1789)

Call your local post office and see if they will give your little ones a tour. Use today's mail to start a stamp collection.

March 19—Missionary/Explorer David Livingstone's Birthday (1813)

Talk about missionaries and what they do. Have your children make cards or pictures to send to a missionary your church supports. It's also a great day to play stuffed animal safari.

March 24—The First Automobile Sold in the U.S. (1898)

Go for a drive to your local car dealership and let your children enjoy looking at all the vehicles.

March 31—The Eiffel Tower Completed (1889)

Challenge your children to build the highest tower they can. Provide some original building materials like empty boxes, pillows, and canned vegetables.

April

April showers bring May flowers. While you are waiting for the rain to stop and the flowers to bloom, try some of these activities.

April 2—Author Hans Christian Andersen's Birthday (1805)

Invite your children to act out the story as you read *The Ugly Duckling*. Help them to create a story of their own.

April 4—First U.S. Flag Approved (1818)

Provide your children with an American flag, or a photo of one. Equip them with paper and red, white, and blue crayons and encourage them to make their own.

April 9—America's First Public Library Established (1833)

Visit the library, of course!

April 20—Make a Quilt Day

Give each child a coloring book page or a sheet of paper. Instruct them to color or draw on the paper. Make sure they color heavily, pressing down hard on the crayons. When they are finished, place the pictures, crayon side down, on a piece of material. Each picture will be a square on your quilt. Using a hot iron, press down on the crayoned picture. The crayons will melt into the fabric and transfer a mirror image onto the material. When all the pictures are ironed on, sew a hem around the material to keep it from fraying and use it as a wall hanging.

April 26—Naturalist J. J. Audubon's Birthday (1785)

Discuss what types of birds visit your backyard. Prepare and set out some tasty treats for your feathered friends.

Birdseed Snacks

For each birdseed snack you will need 1 pinecone, peanut butter, birdseed, string.

This activity is messy, so if it's nice weather, work outside. Have children spread peanut butter all over their pinecone using a spoon. Put the birdseed in a large bowl and allow each child to cover their pinecone with seed by rolling it. Attach a string to each pinecone and hang in a nearby tree.

Edible Bird's Nest

You can make these tasty treats before going on a bird-watching walk. When you get back, they will be ready to eat.

chow mein noodles
1 cup chocolate chips
1 tablespoon shortening
jelly beans
chocolate eggs
marshmallow chicks
peanut butter

Give each child a square of waxed paper to work on. Put the chow mein noodles in a large bowl. Melt the chocolate chips and shortening in the microwave. Stir to combine. Pour the melted chocolate over the chow mein noodles and stir to coat. Place a mound of noodles on each piece of waxed paper. When the chocolate has cooled to the touch, have the children form the mixture into nests. They can decorate their nests using jelly beans, chocolate eggs, and marshmallow chicks. Use peanut butter as "glue."

MAY

It's time to get outdoors again. Pepper your days with walks in the milder temperatures. Remember that any activity you can do inside can probably be done outside as well.

May 1—Mother Goose Day

Help your child memorize some Mother Goose rhymes. Have a recitation after dinner for the family.

May 2—"Peter and the Wolf" Premiered in Moscow (1936)

This wonderful composition is a popular recording in our home. It's a great way to introduce your children to the orchestra. Encourage your children to imagine they are the different characters in the story when they hear the appropriate music.

May 7—Composers Johannes Brahms' (1833) and Peter Tchaikovsky's Birthdays (1840)

These two men graced our world with some of its most beautiful music. Their names conjure up images of lullabies and ballets. Introduce your child to the soothing effects of classical music.

May 14—Lewis and Clark Expedition Began (1804)

This is the day to take a long walk at a preschooler's pace. Pack a snack and see what's new in your neighborhood. Don't rush to get somewhere—just explore.

May 16—Biographers' Day

Help your child tell her story. With a tape recorder running, ask your little one open-ended questions about her life. She will enjoy listening to her view of the world in another ten years.

May 18—Mount St. Helens Erupted (1980)

Have your child build a large mountain out of clay. Make a hole in the top of the mountain large enough to hold a small disposable cup. In the cup, combine a tablespoon of baking soda and a teaspoon of vinegar and watch the volcano erupt.

June

June is the month for fresh fruits and vegetables. If you are able, take advantage of pick-your-own strawberry farms. Get enough to make homemade strawberry jam. When January rolls around, you'll have a delicious taste of summer to enjoy.

Strawberry Freezer Jam

For five cups of jam you will need:

2 pints (1 quart) strawberries
4 cups sugar
1 cup water
1 package powdered fruit pectin

Clean and hull the strawberries. In a large bowl let the children crush them using a potato masher or fork. Stir in sugar and let stand 10 minutes. In a small saucepan combine fruit pectin and water. Heat to boiling and boil for 1 minute, stirring constantly. Pour pectin mixture into fruit mixture. Stir 3 minutes to dissolve most of the sugar. Spoon into clean jars or freezer containers, leaving 1/2 inch of headspace. Cool slightly and cover with tight-fitting lids. Let set overnight or for 24 hours. Store in your freezer for up to one year or in the refrigerator two to three weeks.

June 3—"Casey at the Bat" Published (1888)

Get a copy of this classic poem and read it to your children.

June 8—Ice Cream First Sold in the U.S. (1786)

Make some homemade ice cream.

Tin Can Ice Cream

To make one batch of vanilla ice cream you will need:

1 cup milk
1 cup heavy cream
1/2 cup sugar
1/2 teaspoon vanilla
pinch of salt
rock salt

ice
1 12-ounce coffee can with tight-fitting lid
1 39-ounce coffee can with tight-fitting lid

Mix in a large bowl the milk, cream, sugar, vanilla, and pinch of salt. Stir until sugar is dissolved. Pour the mix into the smaller coffee can and snap the lid on tightly. Set the smaller can inside the larger can and pack crushed ice around it. Sprinkle rock salt over the ice and snap the lid on the larger can.

Have your children roll the can back and forth between them. After about 15 minutes remove the lid on the larger can and drain the water. Open the lid on the smaller can and stir the thickening ice cream mixture. Replace the lid. Add more ice and salt to the larger can and replace its lid. Have the children roll the can for 10 more minutes.

The ice cream will be soft-serve and delicious.

June 12—First Baseball Game Played in the U.S. (1839)

Take the family outside for a friendly game of ball. Serve hotdogs and peanuts for lunch.

JULY

Our favorite July and August activities are playing in the sandbox and the pool. Here are some other activities to try during those hot and hazy days.

July 5—Phineas T. Barnum's Birthday (1810)

P. T. Barnum may be most well known for his circus, but did you know he also owned a clock factory, built several natural history museums, and built the town of Bridgeport, Connecticut? Help your children to create their own museum using their stuffed animals, toys, and knickknacks. Let them take you on a guided tour.

July 7—Chocolate Day; Chocolate Introduced in Europe (1550)

This is the day to enjoy lots of yummy chocolate treats.

Chocolate Brownies

For two dozen brownies you will need:

1 2/3 cups sugar
1 1/2 sticks margarine, melted
2 tablespoons water
2 eggs
2 teaspoons vanilla
1 1/3 cups flour
3/4 cup unsweetened cocoa
1/2 teaspoon baking powder

Preheat oven to 350°. Stir together sugar, melted margarine, and water in a large bowl. Stir in eggs and vanilla. Add flour, cocoa, and baking powder and mix well. Spread into a greased 13 x 9-inch baking pan. Bake 18 to 25 minutes or until toothpick inserted comes out slightly sticky. Cool in pan.

July 9—Doughnut Cutter Invented (1872)

Take a trip to your favorite bakery or doughnut shop!

July 11—Author E. B. White's Birthday (1899)

Begin reading E. B. White's wonderful classic, *Charlotte's Web*. Take the kids to a country fair to see the animals.

July 13—International Puzzle Day

After you have worked a favorite puzzle together, let the kids make their own. For each puzzle you will need 1 piece cardboard, markers or crayons, scissors.

Let each child draw and color a picture on the cardboard. Cut the finished artwork into puzzle pieces. Mix the pieces up and see how long it takes to put it back together.

July 19—Ice Cream Day

Another day devoted to ice cream, hooray! Set up an ice cream sundae fixings bar for dessert tonight. Offer chocolate sauce, strawberry preserves, caramel topping, sprinkles, whipped cream, cherries, bananas, and crushed candy bars. Tailor the choices to your family's tastes.

July 28—Author Beatrix Potter's Birthday (1866)

If you haven't done so already, today is the perfect day to introduce your little ones to Beatrix Potter's delightful classic, *Peter Rabbit.* Enjoy some carrot salad while you do.

Carrot Salad

For six servings you will need:

6 medium carrots
1/2 cup diced apple
1/3 cup raisins
1/2 cup mayonnaise

Grate the carrots by hand or with a food processor. Mix with raisins, apples, and mayonnaise. Chill before serving.

August

August 5—Astronaut Neil Armstrong's Birthday (1930)

In honor of Neil Armstrong's birthday let the kids stay up late. Put blankets in the backyard and watch the stars. Let them imagine what it would be like to fly into space.

August 9—Smokey the Bear's Birthday (1944)

Discuss fire safety with your children. Explain the dangers of playing with matches or the stove. Make sure they know what to do in case of a fire. Practice an escape plan.

August 19—National Aviation Day; Orville Wright's Birthday (1871)

Make paper airplanes and fly them in the backyard. See who comes up with the one that flies the farthest, which one is most original, and which lasts the longest.

August 21—Hawaii Became Fiftieth State (1959)

In honor of our fiftieth state treat your family to pineapple and teach them to do the hula.

Easy Pineapple Upside-Down Cake

1/2 cup brown sugar, firmly packed
1/4 cup margarine or butter, melted
6 canned pineapple slices
6 maraschino cherries (optional)
1/4 cup pineapple juice (you can use the juice from the canned pineapple)
1 box yellow cake mix

Preheat the oven to 350°. In a small bowl combine brown sugar and margarine. Spread in the bottom of a 9-inch round cake pan. Arrange pineapple slices and maraschino cherries over brown sugar mixture. Prepare cake mix according to box directions, but decreasing water by 1/4 cup. Add 1/4 cup pineapple juice to cake mix.

Pour prepared mix into pan over pineapple slices and cherries. Bake 30 to 35 minutes or until toothpick inserted comes out clean. Cool in pan 2 minutes. Invert onto serving plate.

August 24—National Parks Service Established (1916)

Plan a picnic in your local park. You can also check out videos of different National Parks from your library and watch them together.

SEPTEMBER

Summer is over, and older siblings are back at school. Now you can devote some private time to your preschooler. Enjoy!

September 11—Writer O. Henry's Birthday (1862)

Our favorite O. Henry story is "The Gift of the Magi." There are some beautifully illustrated versions available for you to share with your children. Help them think of something they own that they could give up for someone else.

September 13—International Chocolate Day

Chocolate Pretzels

We can never get enough chocolate. For an easy treat of chocolate-dipped pretzels you will need: 1 bag of milk chocolate chips and 1 bag of pretzel rods.

Melt the chocolate chips in a microwave-safe bowl. Let the kids dip one end of the pretzel rods into the chocolate. Lay the coated pretzels to cool and harden on waxed paper before eating. To speed the hardening process, put the coated pretzel rods in the freezer for 5 minutes.

September 14—Francis Scott Key Wrote "The Star Spangled Banner" (1814)

Introduce your preschooler to our national anthem. Talk about the flag and what it means. Teach your little ones the Pledge of Allegiance.

September 19—Walt Disney Produced the First "Talking" Cartoon (1928)

I don't usually recommend watching videos, but today would be a great day to rent a Disney classic like *Snow White* or *Sleeping Beauty.*

September 25—Explorer Balboa Discovered the Pacific Ocean (1513)

If you can't visit the ocean today, bring its atmosphere to you. Let the kids spread towels on the floor, put on bathing suits, and pretend they are at the beach.

OCTOBER

There is so much to do in October. Take advantage of fall activities like pumpkin picking, hayrides, and jumping in huge piles of leaves. It's fun to make a little nest in the middle of a huge leaf pile. Get some blankets, cider, and doughnuts, and have a snack in your comfy leaf pile.

October 23—Athlete Pele's Birthday (1940)

Soccer is a very popular sport for children. After you rake the leaves, gather the kids for a game of soccer on the lawn in honor of the birth of soccer's greatest player.

October 25—Johann Strauss' Birthday (1825)

Strauss was the king of the waltz. Why not teach the little ones this classic dance?

October 27—Navy Day

Gather a fleet of boats and set sail in the bathtub.

November

While November and December are already exciting, activity-filled months, we sometimes need a break from the holiday rush. Try these simple ideas to break up your days.

November 3—Sandwich Day; Sandwich Invented (1762)

Get some different kinds of breads, meats, veggies, and condiments, and set up a sandwich buffet for dinner. Let the kids create their own version of the perfect sandwich. Don't forget the pickles on the side.

November 14—Artist Claude Monet's Birthday (1840)

Monet is Libby's favorite artist. She is so taken by the colors and all the flowers. Why not let your budding artist create a masterpiece on the anniversary of Monet's birth?

November 18—The First Teddy Bear's Birthday (1902)

Place a picnic blanket on the floor, send invitations to all the teddy bears in your house, and have a teddy bear picnic. It's great fun and the cleanup is easy; just shake the blanket outside. Read *Goldilocks and the Three Bears* to your children and their furry friends.

December

December 3—Galileo Perfected the Telescope (1621)

The sky in December is often clear. Wake up your children after dark and take them outside to stargaze. It will be one of those magical moments they will remember all their lives.

December 9—Christmas Cards Created (1843)

Get out the paper, crayons, pencils, and other craft supplies and help your children make their own Christmas cards to send to family and friends.

December 30—Author Rudyard Kipling's Birthday (1865)

Children love Kipling's delightful story *The Jungle Book*. Reading it is a great way to spend a sleepy after-Christmas day.

Make Activities You Plan for Your Family Interesting to You Too

It can be hard to get motivated to plan events for your children. In our adult point of view there are more interesting things to do than play with Matchbox cars or dolls. Children can tell when we are just not into playing with them; find things you can get excited about to share. Insert unique, special occasions into your schedule. It's much more exciting to wake up and say, "Today is Inventors' Day," than to say, "Oh, another Monday." These events will not only bless your family, but you too. Your enthusiasm will be contagious, and you will have more cooperative and appreciative children.

CHAPTER 8

Fun on the Run

WE'VE ALL BEEN in a restaurant at some time enjoying our meal when a child two tables away begins to fuss. In my prechild days it would have annoyed me; now I feel great sympathy for the mother of that child. I know how frustrating it can be when everyone in a doctor's office, grocery store, restaurant, or other public place is looking at you to get your child under control. This chapter is about being prepared for those moments and what to do ahead of time to help minimize them. I can't guarantee these ideas will solve every incidence of fussiness, but having a game plan certainly helps. Like a Girl Scout, moms need to always be prepared.

Dining without Whining

Many restaurants are so busy today that you spend time waiting for a table and then again for your meal. Long before the food is served the children are starving and cranky. One of the best tips I can pass along for parents dining out with their children is to serve them a small, nutritious snack before you head out to eat. When you are seated at the restaurant ask your server to bring water in a child-safe cup and some crackers for your little one to munch on.

Most family restaurants provide young patrons with crayons and a place mat to color, but there is always that one occasion when these items are not offered. Keep a pencil and a small notepad in your bag just in case. Encourage your children to draw a picture of their favorite meal. Teach them how to play tic-tac-toe. You can also doodle on a piece of the notepaper and challenge your child to create a masterpiece out of it. One mom I know learned to do simple origami so she could create disposable toys out of napkins to occupy her children.

Playing the Waiting Game

Moms spend an incredible amount of time with their children in waiting rooms. We visit the pediatrician, the dentist, and the eye doctor. We wait at the photography studio and at school for older siblings. I was at the dentist when I overheard a little boy ask his mom what they were supposed to do before they saw the dentist. She replied, "Sit and wait." "Mommy, my brain is on play. It's too busy to wait," he told her. Preschoolers don't have a pause button. You can take advantage of seemingly "lost time" waiting by helping your child learn and grow.

Waiting rooms are great places to teach your child her address and telephone number. Sing the information using a simple tune such as "Happy Birthday." Review Bible verses. Ask your child to recite his verse standing as still as possible on one foot. Have them practice some basic skills such as tying their shoes or working buttons and zippers on their coats. Your child's kindergarten teacher will be very grateful if your child has mastered these skills.

While we wait for the doctor or dentist I tell my children to think of questions they have for the doctor. I ask them to show me where their eyes, nose, mouth, ears, and other body parts are. In the dentist's waiting room I give them a small mirror and challenge them to count their teeth.

Magazines are ordinarily available in waiting rooms, but they are not usually for children. Using whatever magazine is on hand, let your child search for an assigned picture. Tell your daughter to find all the babies and count them. If she can find more than ten, reward her with a story about when she was a baby. You can also use the magazines for an alphabet search. How many letters of the alphabet can you find in headlines before you need to see the doctor?

Reinforce your child's concept of shapes by asking him to look for items that are square or round. Do you remember the game I Spy? This is a great waiting game. See if your child can guess what you are looking at by giving them clues. If the item your daughter is to guess is her yellow boots say, "I spy with my little eye something yellow." How many clues does she need before she can figure out what the item is?

When we are in a crowded area, such as at a sporting event, theater, or mall, I invite my children to count how many people they see who are wearing hats or who have blond hair or some other characteristic. On a trip to the store I tell them to carefully notice everything around them. When we are in the car on the way home, whoever can give me the most detailed description of the store gets a special story.

There are times when grocery shopping is quite a challenge with little ones. Take advantage of the store giveaways. My grocery store will give children shopping with their parents a slice of cheese at the deli, a cookie at the bakery, and an apple in the produce section. Nicholas is usually happy to munch his way through the aisles.

Give your children pictures of items you need to purchase or coupons to hold. Explain that you are on a treasure hunt and the coupons are your child's clues. They can help you shop by keeping an eye out for these "treasures." If you are teaching your child to count, ask her to keep track of how many items you are buying. It may take you longer to get through the store, but it will be more fun.

Pack a Survival Kit

Having the right supplies available can make or break your day. Try to keep special toys, books, and snacks for different situations.

Keep some nonperishable snacks and water bottles in the car. Hungry children are not the most cooperative, and you can spend a small fortune stopping at fast-food restaurants for snacks—not to mention the fact that fast food is not the healthiest choice for growing children. Our favorite on-the-go snacks include small bags of cereal, pretzel rods, animal crackers, cereal bars, granola bars, and snack crackers. Try to choose low-sugar snacks to keep children from getting hyper.

Most prepackaged trail mixes contain potential choking hazards for small children. We created our own using Nick and Libby's favorite cereals, pretzels, animal crackers, dried fruit, raisins, and on special trips, chocolate chips. Mix up your own brand of trail mix with your little one before your next outing.

It's also very helpful to keep some fun kids' music cassettes in the car. Music is a wonderful way to set a mood. Sing-along tapes and classical music have soothed my children on many long journeys. Visit your local library and borrow some books on tape. Listening to a story in the car is a great way to help your child develop better listening skills while keeping them occupied. We have enjoyed *The Indian in the Cupboard*, *Cinderella*, and many Adventures in Odyssey. Focus on the Family also offers wonderful radio theater. These tapes include C. S. Lewis classics like *The Lion, the Witch, and the Wardrobe* and *The Horse and His Boy*. One family I know purchased a personal tape player and headset for each of their children. Each child is able to listen to their favorite audiocassette. This mom felt the quiet car ride was worth the investment.

Drawing paper, coloring books, and colored pencils are great travel tools. Your child can keep an outing journal by drawing pictures of places you go. We use colored pencils in the car as opposed to crayons because crayons will melt in hot weather. (Believe me, getting melted crayon off the car's upholstery is a difficult task!) Be sure to keep a pencil sharpener with a shavings collection cap in the glove compartment to keep pencils sharp.

Wherever you go, it's good to have some quiet, self-contained toys. Look for items such as Etch-a-Sketches, Magna Doodles, a few wooden blocks in a plastic container, dolls or a favorite stuffed toy, and durable books to take along to the doctor's office, restaurant, church meeting, or Grandma's house. Children can't be expected to occupy themselves for long without something to play with.

Play clay stored inside a plastic container is another traveling boredom buster. Store in an empty margarine tub or other small plastic container. Your child can play with the clay inside the plastic container to prevent clay crumbs being scattered everywhere.

Nonhardening Clay

2 cups flour
1 cup salt
1 teaspoon cream of tartar
2 tablespoons oil
1 teaspoon food coloring
2 cups water

Mix all the ingredients in a saucepan. Cook over medium heat, stirring constantly, until the dough leaves the sides of the pan. Remove from the pan. When cool to the touch, knead the clay for a few minutes. Stored in a plastic container, the clay should last for months.

Magnetic Tic-Tac-Toe

Another great on-the-go toy is a magnetic game board. You can easily make one for your child using a cookie tin, paint pens, magnetic sheet, hot glue, and scissors.

Paint and decorate the outside of the cookie tin if you like. Trace the outline of the cookie tin lid onto a magnetic sheet. Cut the outline just inside the line so that the magnet is slightly smaller than the tin lid. Using paint pens, draw a tic-tac-toe game board on the magnetic sheet. Fit the magnetic sheet inside the bottom of the cookie tin. Make playing pieces by cutting the magnetic sheet into ten squares. Decorate five with *X* and five with *O*. This same idea can be used to make a checker or chess board when your children are older.

When we are in the car, everyone feels free to sing loud and heartily. When I was growing up my dad taught us all his favorite tunes while traveling to my grandmother's house each Sunday. I am now teaching my children those same old standards, such as "You Are My Sunshine" and "Harvest Moon." Start the tradition of family sing-alongs in your vehicle.

Storytelling is a wonderful on-the-way-home travel boredom buster. Mom can begin a story the kids know well, such as *The Three Little Pigs*, and let the children take turns telling part of the story in their own words. It's fun to hear their interpretations of age-old classics.

I always make it a point to keep a set of extra clothes, a blanket, a towel, a first-aid kit, and extra diapers and wipes in the trunk of my car. I choose clothing that is comfortable, like a sweat suit, that can serve as pajamas on a late night out. When we get home, I don't have to wake my children to change them for bed. The extra supplies don't take much room, and the items have proved invaluable on many occasions.

On one such occasion, a moms' group picnic in a park, the children were drawn to the creek. Although we were careful to supervise the little ones, my friend's daughter Emily fell in. She was upset, soaked, and uncomfortable. I pulled out my towel and spare clothes. Her mom was able to dry her off and change her in the bathroom. Instead of having to leave, mom and daughter were able to stay and enjoy the rest of the day.

Plan a Pit Stop

Children cannot keep their exuberant energy under control all the time. They need time to burn off some of their energy in an acceptable way. Each day give them some time and space to be children. When you are on a long car trip, break it up by stopping at a park for a fifteen-minute break. We often went to a McDonald's playplace after a meeting at church to let Nick and Libby climb and run and have some fun. It's a great reward for their good behavior, and exercise is so important for a child's well-being! Take time to romp with them. It will refresh you after a long morning too.

Be Prepared and Plan Ahead

If you plan ahead for outings and times you need your child to occupy themselves, you will find it is much easier for your child to behave. If we let our children know our expectations, keep in mind their limitations, and equip them properly, outings will be much more pleasant. Nicholas and Libby know we can do more fun things with them if they cooperate when we need to accomplish "adult" tasks. Let your children know you appreciate their cooperation and good behavior.

CHAPTER 9

Fantastic Faith Builders

I WOULD BE REMISS if I closed this Little Book for Busy Moms without passing on ideas for celebrating the ultimate gift you can give yourself and your children. A strong relationship with Jesus our Savior is the most valuable source of joy for my family. If you wish for your children to be blessed by this relationship, you need to actively guide them. Through activities like the ones in this chapter my children have developed a greater awareness of God's presence in their lives. This awareness has blessed not only them, but my husband and me as well.

Many people don't realize that being a Christian is fun. It is exciting. It is comforting and peaceful. It is eternal joy. How do we bless our children with this saving knowledge? The task doesn't have to be as daunting as some think.

Prayer

Begin with prayer. Pray regularly for and with your children. In order for children to develop a relationship with God, they need to learn to talk to him. When you pray with your children, you are training them for their own conversations with God. Make prayer a natural part of your day. Every prayer is important to God.

Schedule prayer time into your daily activities. Many families pray before meals and at bedtime. We also pray before we drive off in our car as a family or whenever Jim and I must leave our children with a baby-sitter. We have developed a habit, through our prayers, of reassuring our children and ourselves of God's protection and love whenever we need to travel or be apart.

Make your children comfortable with spontaneous prayer. Whenever we hear the wail of a siren, we stop and say a short prayer for the emergency workers and the people who need their assistance. If a family member gets good news or accomplishes a difficult task, we praise God right away. This doesn't have to be long and involved. Simply saying, "Thank you, Lord, for blessing Libby in her dance class," is enough.

One winter I had an accident coming home from a meeting at church. Nicholas and Libby were both in the car with me. I skidded on some ice and totaled our vehicle, but God preserved us. When the car stopped, Nicholas, then four years old, said, "See, Mommy, God always hears our prayers."

A year later I had to pick Nicholas up at a church about ten miles from our house. It was an awful winter day and the snow was coming down hard. I must admit, I became a wreck behind the wheel. My car was fishtailing and sliding all the way. Libby silently listened to me pray out loud through my tears. When we finally arrived at the church to pick up Nick, he confidently hopped into his seat. Crying, I told the children I didn't think I could get us home all alone. Libby reminded me of how God had taken care of us before, and Nick told me we were not alone. They also said they would pray us home. For the next forty-five minutes my four- and five-year-old children prayed out loud. They prayed around curves and hills. They thanked God for people we knew along our route, just in case we got stuck. Their prayers comforted me and allowed the Holy

Spirit to guide me. I was truly blessed by my children. In my time of weakness, God used them to hold me up.

Encourage you children to have their own conversations with God. Begin with teaching your child prayers from Scripture such as the Lord's Prayer and the Twenty-third Psalm. You will be surprised how quickly children can memorize Scripture. It takes patience on your part and much repetition, but it is a blessing to you and to them.

We have used the "ACTS" style of prayer (Adoration, Confession, Thanksgiving, Supplication) to guide our children through their prayers. I ask each child to tell God how much they love him and why. Then I ask them if there is anything they did or said today for which they need to say they are sorry. Next I have them thank God for at least three things he has blessed them with. Finally, each child prays for something for someone else and something for themselves.

Prayer Journals

Purchase small notepads for each of your children. Ask them to tell you the names of all the friends and family members for whom they think they should be praying. Put these names in the notebook. Each evening, encourage your child to pray for the next person on their list. This helps your children focus their prayers more specifically and prevents them from repeating the same prayers each evening.

Christmas Card Prayers

When the Christmas season ends, don't toss or store all those Christmas greetings. Place them in a basket, and one evening each week when you have your prayer time take a card from the top of the stack. Pray for the family or friend that sent that Christmas greeting. You can also have the children make cards to send to that person to let them know you are praying for them.

Prayer Pretzels

This is a fun activity to help your children remember to pray at all times. Tell them the following story while you prepare the pretzels:

Monks are men who live in a place called a monastery. They spend all their time praying and never leave their homes. In Germany, during the fourteenth and fifteenth centuries, monks always bowed and covered their heads with the hood of their robes. They also folded their arms across their chests to make a cross to remind people of Jesus' suffering for our sins. They needed a way to support themselves financially, so they baked and sold little breads called pretzels. The monks shaped the pretzels to look like their folded arms to remind people to pray continually.

Prayer Pretzels

To make a batch of pretzels you will need:

1 package of yeast
1 1/2 cups warm water
1 teaspoon salt
1 teaspoon sugar
4 cups flour
1 egg, beaten
coarse salt

Preheat oven to 425°. Dissolve the yeast in the warm water. Add the salt and sugar to the yeast mixture. Blend in the flour. Have the children knead the dough until it is smooth. Break the dough into small pieces. Show the children how to roll the dough into ropes and twist them into shape. Brush the pretzels with the beaten egg. Sprinkle with coarse salt and bake 12 to 15 minutes.

Blessings

When Nicholas and Libby were very small, I read an article about blessing your children. I realized this was something Jim and I should be doing for our children. We began that night. When it was time for bed, we tucked each child in, laid a hand on each of their heads, and spoke a blessing on them individually. We have done it ever since. If for some reason we are not home when they go to bed, we go into their rooms later and bless them while they are sleeping. We created our blessing based on Scripture and what we felt we wanted God to bestow on our children.

Think carefully about what you want for your children, then create a blessing for them. Blessings are much more than a bedtime ritual; when you bless your children, the blessings will come back tenfold. We say the same blessing every night: "May the Lord bless you and keep you, make his face shine upon you, and give you peace, wisdom, self-control, and joy. May he always protect you and draw you close to him."

Nicholas and Libby have come to depend upon this blessing as a token of security and a sign of our love for them day in and day out. It is one of the simplest and most powerful ways I know to give my children a daily encounter with God's love and power.

Bible Stories and Activities

There are many fun ways to teach your children Bible stories and principles. The simplest is to purchase a good Bible storybook to use for bedtime stories each evening or during some other cuddle time.

We have used *The Tiny Tots Bible Storybook* by John and Kim Walton and *The Early Reader's Bible* by V. Gilbert Beers. Eventually we graduated to the NIV Bible. Children love stories. Use all your storytelling talents to make them memorable. Using different voices for different characters and changing the inflection of your voice to mirror what's going on will really draw them in. Ask your children questions about what happened in the story and how they would feel if they were the people involved.

It's great fun to use stuffed animals to tell Bible stories. Nick's stuffed lion has been the narrator for Daniel and the lions' den, and Libby's toy horse has been Balaam's donkey. Hearing the stories from the animal's point of view is silly, but it helped our children remember the lessons we were trying to teach.

It's fun to have your children act out a Bible story as you read it. The story of Esther is very popular in our house. We invite over extended family for our play. Libby loves playing the beautiful and brave queen. The entire family gets into the act. Dad plays Haman, and we encourage the audience to boo him and cheer wildly for Esther and Mordecai.

Use props to help tell Bible stories. Nicholas has a Fisher-Price farm set that has been our nativity set for years. We purchased small plastic figures of Mary, Joseph, baby Jesus, and the wise men at our local

Christian bookstore. Nicholas and Libby have reenacted the birth of Christ many times with those toys.

Look for other figures in your Christian bookstore that will encourage your children to "play" Bible stories. We have seen figures for Daniel and the lions' den, Esther, and the Resurrection. I have also made clothes out of material scraps so dolls Libby already has can become some of the characters in our Bible stories.

Another great Bible story prop is a flannelboard and figures. You can purchase them at school supply stores or Christian bookstores. You can also use the back of a couch as a flannelboard. We have found felt shapes adhere just fine there. Either buy pieces of felt and make your own figures or purchase premade ones from Christian suppliers. Let the children set up the figures and move them around as the story progresses.

Whenever you can couple a story with an action, you reinforce it. We once helped Nicholas and Libby decorate a cardboard refrigerator box to look like a whale. We read the story of Jonah while huddled inside the box. Being in a dark, cramped place helped them experience some of what Jonah might have felt. You can use a refrigerator box to create an ark for the story of Noah or a ship to tell the story about when Jesus calmed the stormy sea. The story of David and Goliath can be reinforced by drawing an outline of a giant on the sidewalk with chalk. Let the children lie down beside it and trace their outline. They can compare the size of the giant to their own size.

Hide-and-seek is a great game to illustrate some biblical truths. Tell your children to hide while you count to ten. If your children are like mine, finding them is not a challenge, but this will still work even if you can't locate them. When the game is over tell your children the story of Jonah. He could not hide from God and neither can we. Read Psalm 139:7–12. God can find us no matter where we go.

We have used trick birthday candles to illustrate God's love. These candles do not go out unless you put them in a glass of water. Light the candle and challenge your child to blow it out. Tell them the candle's flame is like God's love. Ask them to name things they think will cause God to stop loving them and then try to blow out the flame. There is nothing we can do to "put out" the love God has for us.

Help your children learn the story of Jesus' resurrection using the cookie recipe below. They need to be started before bedtime, so we usually make them the night before Easter.

Resurrection Cookies

1 cup of nuts (we like pecans)
3 egg whites
1 teaspoon vinegar
1 cup sugar

pinch of salt
wooden spoon
large resealable plastic bag
masking tape
Bible

Preheat oven to 300°. Place the nuts in a resealable plastic bag and have your children pound the nuts into small pieces using a wooden spoon. While they are doing this read John 19:1–2. Point out that Jesus was beaten by Roman soldiers.

Have your children smell the vinegar before putting it into a large mixing bowl. Read John 19:28–30. Ask the children if they would like to drink vinegar when they wanted water to quench their thirst. Add egg whites to the vinegar.

Sprinkle a few grains of salt into your hand so the children can taste them. Add a pinch to the bowl. Read Luke 23:27. Explain that Jesus' friends cried salty tears because he had to suffer on the cross.

Add one cup of sugar. Read Romans 5:8. Tell your children that the sweetest part of this story is that Jesus died to give us eternal life. Beat the mixture with a mixer on high speed for 12 to 15 minutes, until stiff peaks form.

Read Isaiah 1:18. Tell the children that white represents purity. We become clean and pure when we confess our sins to Jesus.

Fold in the crushed nuts and drop mounds of the mixture onto a waxed-paper-covered cookie sheet. The mounds will look like little rocks. Read Matthew 27:57–60 and talk about the huge rock that covered the doorway of Jesus' tomb.

Put the cookies in the oven and turn the oven off. Let the children seal the closed oven door with masking tape so no one can open it. Read Matthew 27:62–66 and explain that Jesus' tomb was sealed and guarded so no one could enter it. Put the children to bed.

The next morning have them take the tape off the oven and open the door. Look at the cracked surface of the cookies. Let them take a bite. The cookies are hollow. Read Luke 24:1–12 and rejoice. Jesus' tomb was empty! Tell the children, "He is risen."

When you choose toys, videos, audiotapes, and books for your children, keep in mind their spiritual training. Choose things that will support your Christian beliefs. Videos like Veggie Tales, Psalty, and the Donut Man are upbeat and fun, and teach a Christian message. Puzzles with biblical themes teach coordination just as well as secular puzzles do. Bible verses are memorized even more quickly when set to music, and there are plenty of tapes to choose from. Scripture and hymns have soothed our children to sleep on many fussy evenings. Try audio cassettes by Michael Card or Bob Carlisle. Some of our favorite books are *In Case You Ever Wonder* by Max Lucado, *I'd Choose You* by John Trent, *Let's Make Jesus Happy* by Mack Thomas, and *Christian Mother Goose Rock-a-Bye Bible* by Marjorie Ainsborough Decker. If you don't have a well-stocked Christian bookstore in your area, you can purchase items through Christian Book Distributors. Call 978-977-5005 for their catalog.

SERVICE

Look for ways your family can be missionaries where you are. There are plenty of opportunities to serve God right from your home or community. Let your children help you bake bread or cookies for a local food bank. Call ahead to find out when the food bank distributes food so you can drop off your baked goods that day.

Christmas offers many opportunities to serve others. Each year our family participates in Samaritan's Purse's Operation Christmas Child. We take the children to the store and help them each pick out enough toiletries, small toys and books, school supplies, socks, T-shirts, and gum or candy to fill a shoe box. At home we wrap the shoe boxes and lids separately with Christmas paper and fill them with the items the children have chosen. Nicholas and Libby often draw pictures or write notes to accompany their gifts. We pray for the child who will receive each shoe box, and bring the boxes to the designated drop-off center. Each box also requires a five-dollar donation to help defray shipping costs. Samaritan's Purse then distributes these boxes to children in poverty-stricken or war-ravaged countries around the world. You can contact Samaritan's Purse at P.O. Box 3000, Boone, NC 28607.

Some hospitals welcome donations of Christmas cookies to distribute to families who have children in the pediatric or neonatal units. We have also donated Christmas goodies to a local nursing home. Friends of ours make place mats for nursing home residents for Christmas or Thanksgiving. Have the children design a place mat on white paper, then take the place mats to a quick-copy center and have them copy as many as the nursing home needs.

Another great way to teach your children to reach beyond themselves with God's love is to adopt a missionary family. Ask your pastor for the name and address of a missionary family that may have a child near your children's ages. Send them a letter with a photo of your family to introduce yourselves. Explain that your family wants to bless them and pray for them. Many missionary families welcome this support. Periodically send them "care packages."

When living in another country, you miss little items you could easily get in the United States, like chocolate or a magazine subscription. Ask your missionary family what they miss most. On a map or globe, show your child where these missionaries live and where you live. Learn about the country in which they are serving. When the family comes home on furlough, if convenient for them, invite them over for a home-cooked meal and fellowship. We once hosted dinner for a family serving in Kenya. It was quite a remarkable evening for our entire family. The stories they told of serving God on the "front lines" were an incredible testimony.

Christian Character

I try to *disciple* my children so that I don't have to *discipline* them as much. I look for teachable moments to develop their characters. Often action is much more effective than lectures. I also look for ways they can show, rather than tell, they understand. If Nicholas hurts or offends Libby, he must ask her for forgiveness for a specific indiscretion. Saying "I'm sorry" is not sufficient. Maybe he's sorry he got caught; maybe it's just words. In return, Libby must grant forgiveness. Nicholas must also perform some act of service for his sister. He may have to make her bed for her or clean up the toys himself.

(All of this works the other way when Libby is the offending party.) Both children need to model Christian character. One learns to be responsible for their actions, and one learns to have a forgiving heart. These are both invaluable lessons.

Use a package of their favorite cookies or treats to teach your children to live their faith, not just talk about it. Tell the children you are going to give them their favorite treat in a few minutes, but first they need to tell you about the treat. What does it smell like, feel like, look like, and taste like? Let them answer all your questions. When they are finished, serve the snack. Ask the children why eating the snack is better than talking about the snack. Tell them it is the same way with our belief in Jesus. We can talk about Jesus, but talking doesn't give us the same benefits as actually having Jesus in our lives. We have to live our faith to get all the blessings Jesus has for us. Discuss the blessings your family has experienced. If your children have not accepted Jesus as their Savior yet, now is a great time to invite them to do so.

Look for special moments to point out God's love, provision, and handiwork to your children. Throughout this book you will note occasions to acknowledge God. When you explore your garden, gaze at a starry sky, or tell your child your life stories, do it from a godly perspective. Let your child hear you thanking God for all the wonders and blessings around you.

Take the time to develop a strong relationship with Jesus yourself. Through this relationship not only will you have eternal life, but you will have the power of the Holy Spirit to help you be the best mother you can be. What better blessing can we give our little ones than the joy of the Lord? As your children see you grow in the Lord, they will want to know him better too. As you and your children grow spiritually, you will find parenting gets easier. It becomes fun and purposeful. You will find your creativity abounding and your children showing a more teachable spirit.

Always remember that God is your parenting partner and loves your child even more than you do. I need to lean on this truth so many times during my mothering journey. Children take up so much of our time and energy. Learn to see God through the gifts of your children instead of in spite of them.

It is my prayer that through this Little Book for Busy Moms you and your family are able to grow closer to each other and to God—and have fun, memorable moments doing it. Life is an exciting adventure and a blessing—enjoy it!

Recipes and Ideas Index

About This Busy Mom

BARBARA VOGELGESANG HAS BEEN speaking, performing, and clowning for fifteen years. She has toured with Ringling Bros. and Barnum & Bailey Circus and performed throughout the U.S., Canada, and Japan. Barbara and her husband, Jim, are the proud parents of Nicholas, Libby, and Sarah. She is a CLASS graduate (Christian Leaders, Authors, Speakers Services) and holds a journalism degree from St. John's University in New York City. Barbara has attended Ringling Bros. and Barnum & Bailey's Clown College and worked in the public relations departments of Estee Lauder, Madison Square Garden, and Ringling Bros. and Barnum & Bailey Circus. She now resides in beautiful, rural Pennsylvania.

MOPS stands for Mothers of Preschoolers, a program designed to encourage mothers with children under school age through relationships and resources. These women come from different backgrounds and lifestyles, yet have similar needs and a shared desire to be the best mothers they can be!

A MOPS group provides a caring, accepting atmosphere for today's mother of preschoolers. Here she has an opportunity to share concerns, explore areas of creativity, and hear instruction that equips her for the responsibilities of family and community. The MOPS group also includes MOPPETS, a loving, learning experience for children.

Approximately 2,700 groups meet in churches throughout the United States, Canada, and 19 other countries, to meet the needs of more than 100,000 women. Many more mothers are encouraged by MOPS resources, including *MOMSense* radio and magazine, MOPS' web site, and publications such as this book.

Find out how MOPS International can help you become part of the MOPS♥to♥Mom Connection.

MOPS International
P.O. Box 102200
Denver, CO 80250-2200
Phone 1-800-929-1287 or 303-733-5353
E-mail: Info@MOPS.org
Web site: http://www.MOPS.org
To learn how to start a MOPS group,
call 1-888-910-MOPS.
For MOPS products call The MOPShop
1-888-545-4040.

7.01